THE CANINE KINGDOM OF SCENT

Fun Activities Using Your Dog's Natural Instincts

Anne Lill Kvam

Wenatchee, Washington U.S.A.

The Canine Kingdom of Scent
Fun Activities Using Your Dog's Natural Instincts
Anne Lill Kvam

Dogwise Publishing
A Division of Direct Book Service, Inc.
403 South Mission Street, Wenatchee, Washington 98801
509-663-9115, 1-800-776-2665
www.dogwisepublishing.com / info@dogwisepublishing.com

First published in Norway in 2005 as *Nesearbeid for Hund*

Cover design: Brittney Kind
Interior design: Lindsay Peternell
Interior photographs: Annika Petrén, Lydia Zivkovic, Bjørn Owe Holmberg, Anne Lill Kvam, Siri Møller, Silvia Föller, Gerd Köhler, Turid Sunde, Esa Viitala, Carl Otto Samuelsen.

Limits of Liability and Disclaimer of Warranty:
The author and publisher shall not be liable in the event of incidental or consequential damages in connection with, or arising out of, the furnishing, performance, or use of the instructions and suggestions contained in this book.

ISBN 978-1-929242-72-6

Library of Congress Cataloging-in-Publication Data
Kvam, Anne Lill, 1960-
   The canine kingdom of scent : fun activities using your dog's natural instincts / Anne Lill Kvam.
       p. cm.
   Includes bibliographical references.
   ISBN 978-1-929242-72-6
   1. Dogs--Training. 2. Dogs--Sense organs. 3. Smell. 4. Games for dogs.
I. Title.
   SF431.K83 2011
   636.7'0887--dc23
                                         2011022048
Printed in the U.S.A.

More praise for *The Canine Kingdom of Scent*

This book is one of my favorites and is required reading for my trainer students. It could easily be one of your favorites, too! It certainly is a one-of-a-kind book on this subject.

Anne Lill has been a treasured colleague and friend for years, and I have enjoyed watching her develop her special interest in nosework on all levels. She has had success in working with new dog owners with no ambition other than having fun with their dogs as well as with people wanting to train advanced scent-discrimination tasks like mine-detection, finding peanut oil in food for allergic people, and many, many other variations of using a dog's incredible nose. She has learned that using the nose is motivation in itself; no other motivation for the dog is needed.

With a background in search and rescue, mine-detection in Africa, ID tracking and other areas of nosework, Anne Lill also enjoys the small things everybody can do with their dogs on a daily basis and making a dog's life so much more meaningful and happy. Her students love the way she teaches and makes the dog's work fun. Anne Lill has nosework workshops and camps all over Europe, and has also been to the US, Canada and Japan. She is a much treasured speaker in many seminars and conferences.

This book will help you get started doing nosework with your dog—and your dog will love you for it. For those of who already do nosework with your dog, you will find new, better and easier ways of doing it, as creativity is one of the hallmarks of Anne Lill's training methods. And, best of all, your dog does not need to be "obedient" or know anything at all about nosework. Just read the book and get started!

Turid Rugaas, author of *On Talking Terms With Dogs, My Dog Pulls!,* and *Barking, the Sound of a Language.*

TABLE OF CONTENTS

INTRODUCTION

This book became a reality after many years of teaching classes for dogs and their owners around the world. What I teach are fun and simple nosework activities for dogs, mainly tracking and scent discrimination. My students range from pet owners to professional dog trainers to search and rescue people, customs officials and police officers. Almost everywhere I teach, my students ask if I have written a book yet—and now I have!

While my professional focus is on various kinds of nosework, the real theme of my work with and about dogs is a passion to learn more about them as individuals and as a species, which has led me to a greater respect for their needs, natural language and behavior. The more we ask questions about a dog's habits and instincts, the more we learn about his behavior—and the better trainers we become.

For me, the renewal of my childhood wonder for each animal's individuality and personality occurred through an entertaining but strenuous friendship with Chico, a little Vervet monkey, who lived with me in Angola. In order to train him to do something, I had to study his behavior to discover his likes and dislikes and what made him react this way or that way. After two weeks of training and living together, there came a major test: I let him off leash for the first time. The young monkey rushed like a tiny, furry blizzard to the top of a eucalyptus tree 90 to 120 feet high and vanished. After a while, I regained my breath and followed my training plan. I called, "Chico, come." From the tree tops, Chico gave a screech of recognition and came scurrying and jumping back to collect his strawberry!

Little Chico, the mind opening monkey.

The training methods described in this book are all free of physical punishment and unpleasantness. I prefer to plan the training so the dog, by herself, will choose to do what I want. It is up to you and me to make sure the pay-off for the dog is motivating enough so the likelihood that she will repeat any desired behavior increases. In the art of dog training, many things can happen, and quick improvisations are needed. This makes it necessary to observe each dog to find out what makes her do what we ask. Because of this, you may have to make your own little adjustments to some of my methods, or "recipes" as I like to call them. But do not fall for the temptation to help her solve a problem. Rather, devise an entirely new task for your dog that is slightly easier. Remember to always set your dog (and yourself) up for success!

I hope you and your dog will have many wonderful times together as a result of reading this book.

Anne Lill and Chico, the monkey that trained her so well.

CHAPTER 1

The Kingdom of Scent

When did you last sense the smell of water? My late dog, Troll, could smell water from a long distance. Troll could also hear water, especially when the water was in the form of a cheerful and tempting creek or a waterfall. Of course, I can hear waterfalls, too, but not as far away as she could. On the other hand, Troll could not see people standing still in the distance, although I can. In fact, someone could hide from Troll simply by standing motionless next to a tree in the distance. Troll could only spot the person if he moved.

Troll, the Poodle who taught me so very much.

One day, Troll sat in a chair in my house and barked as she looked out the window. None of us humans in the house could see anything suspicious. But Troll was persistent, and eventually we saw, on the slope about 90 yards away, some roe deer who were moving about between the trees. Were it not for their white tails, none of us humans would have seen the deer, even though Troll could easily see them moving about.

Just like us, dogs can see, smell, hear, taste and feel. All of us who share our lives with dogs have noticed, however, that some of their senses are, in many ways, superior to ours—especially their sense of smell. Their marvellous scenting ability has been put to good use by people for decades. Dogs have long been used to search for people lost in avalanches or forests. Dogs can detect landmines, and you may have heard of dogs searching for truffles in Europe or seen Beagles sniffing luggage at airports in the US, Canada, New Zealand or Australia. Many dogs have learned to find Chanterelle mushrooms for their owners or to back-track the route of a day's walk to fetch something mom lost on a walk. Dogs have also learned to use their sense of smell to pick out an owner's car keys from a pile of many keys.

A new area in which dogs use their sense of smell is in detecting cancer on human patients. The dog sniffs the patient (or a urine or tissue sample) and marks if any cancer cells are present. Fantastic! Apparently, this ability has been known for centuries. A student from a camp in Canada told me he read that using dogs to smell for illness was a practice dating back two to four thousand years. One temple had dogs and once a dog had pointed out an infected area, surgeons would perform surgery. Later, the temple was destroyed and the knowledge disappeared.

How good is a dog's olfactory sense?

Laboratory work conducted by Mechem, a contraband and mine detection company in South Africa, has shown a dog's nose is capable of recognizing molecules as low as a concentration of 10^{-18}. When I first heard that, I had no idea what it meant. The scientist who told me about this was kind and understanding, and explained it for me in a way I could understand. Imagine a beach 1500 feet long, 150 feet wide and 40 inches deep. On this beach, a dog can find two grains of sand that smell differently. Incredible, isn't it?

Dogs I trained in Angola could find land mines hidden 15 inches under the ground that were placed more than 10 years ago. A South African colleague told me of a case where a dog was able to sense a mine which turned out to be 100 feet away from where the dog was. And still we continue to wonder over Rambo's restlessness when a bitch a couple miles away is in heat…

No training needed!

A blind lady passed my house one day, and she told me the story of her late guide dog who would occasionally prevent her from leaving the house. After a couple of times, she realized it would happen only before she was about to have a diabetic fit. She called the guide dog school to ask how they taught this training, only to learn that they had absolutely no idea what she was talking about. The dog had learned to sense a diabetic fit all by herself. There are many similar stories of what dogs are capable of. My experience is that the limitations of the dog's sense of smell, and how to use it, remains in the human brain.

We will never fully comprehend a dog's sense of smell.

CHAPTER 2

Taking Advantage of Natural Behavior

How can we take advantage of a dog's incredible scenting ability and other traits and drives inherited from the wolf to train more effectively and to give her a fuller life? One thing to keep in mind is that while dogs today are quite different from wolves in many ways, they still possess many of the instincts and behaviors that have been passed down to them from their wild predator ancestors.

The "cheapest" food: How your dog prioritizes her senses

A wolf's deepest concern is staying alive. Therefore, they want to obtain as much food as possible while spending as little energy as needed in order to obtain it. The same is true for a dog. Despite their sense of smell, dogs—like humans—actually orient themselves first by vision. Why? Because the "cheapest" food is the closest one, the one that can be seen. If nothing edible is visible, the dog (wolf) will listen for potential prey. Only if neither of these two senses lead to a meal will the dog put her olfactory sense into gear.

Once a dog does begin to use her scenting abilities, she still is searching for the "cheapest" alternative, one that saves her energy. So the first technique she will try will be to sniff the wind for any information. Only if that fails will she get to work putting her nose to the ground and begin sniffing for a track.

Don't forget this when you plan your training. If you want the dog to solve a task using her nose, you have to eliminate any possibilities of her solving the problem by sight or hearing. It can be very annoying for people trying to get their dogs to do nosework when the dog gets distracted by what she can see or hear.

The modern dog inherited scent discrimination skills from the wolf who needed to know what kind of animal it was hunting. Likewise, a dog should be able to smell the difference between tracks left by a moose, hare, fox or another dog. Depending on her motivation, the canine will choose one of the tracks, keeping the "cheapest" concept in mind. If she is hungry and alone she will probably track the hare. If she is hungry and has company, she may track the moose. A lonely dog with a full stomach may choose to follow the dog track. However, if she is fed and satisfied, she is most likely to refrain from doing anything at all!

Following moose tracks in the snow.

The benefits of nosework

Most of our modern pet or working dogs have their meals served by us and don't have to exert or expose themselves to danger while searching for food. While many dogs get sufficient walks, exercise, and maybe even some training, they do not get enough stimulation of their innate senses and abilities. A lot of the training we do with our dogs includes speed, excitement, precision and control, but very few activities require calmness and concentration.

By contrast, nosework requires calm concentration and involves stimulation of several of a dog's innate abilities. Many students from my courses have reported back that, in general, their dog's cooperation has improved, and the relationship between the dog and owner has been strengthened through nosework training. In many cases, an additional benefit noted is that performance in other disciplines, such as obedience competitions, improves. This phenomenon may be enlightened by the understanding of the term dynamic or "situational leadership" (Bru and Kittelsen, 2002). Briefly, situational leadership means that the one having the special skills needed in a particular situation takes the leadership role—and in nosework that is the dog. The owner trusts the dog to follow the scent and the dog trusts the owner in other situations. Both halves of the partnership have their own talents. This management structure is dynamic in that whoever takes the lead (dog or owner) depends on the situation. This type of relationship leads both dog and human to better performance and cooperation and builds mutual trust.

In the end, it appears that the limits to deploying a dog's olfactory sense remain inside the human brain. We simply do not understand the full extent or reach of this terrific tool, and thus are unable to see all the possible uses. But my little dog Tramp, you think, is neither going to find land mines, guard the border against intruders or sniff out cancer cells, so what has all this to do with me or him? Both dog and owner can have lots of fun learning some of the following nosework exercises and using them in daily life. Some "recipes," as I like to call them, are simple and may be trained at home, indoors or in the garden, and others are more complex. My intention is to have something on the menu for everybody. Maybe you will decide to try out more of them after first having tested out some of the exercises you find easiest.

Nosework is fun for both you and your dog.

CHAPTER 3

What You Need to Know to Get Started

Many people believe that the demands made on the dog are the most critical aspects of focused training like nosework. I do not fully agree. First and foremost, it is the demands on *yourself* that need your attention. You must have lots of patience, be highly systematic and be very determined to reach your goals. And, frankly, you must be stubborn! Training of dogs (and other animals) is fun and will bring you joy, but it is never a simple progression. You must deal with stagnation as well as regression in your progress, at least now and then.

Here is my list of what you will need to train your dog in nosework. Note that the first three items relate to you, the trainer:

- Patience.
- An ability to be systematic.
- Sufficient motivation and stubbornness to stick to your plan.
- Knowledge of the dog: how dogs learn; how you can make your dog happy (i.e., which rewards work best); and what limitations, if any, your dog has regarding health, physical abilities, mental strength, etc.
- High value treats (treats your dog *really* enjoys).
- Toys.
- Harness.

- Short (about 9 feet) and long (25 to 40 feet) leash for some of the exercises.

- Something to search for when doing scent discrimination (details will be covered in the following chapters).

As long as your dog is healthy and has no injuries that hinder her, you can train the dog for almost any purpose. Not all become champions, but every dog can learn something and do it well. Adjust your expectations and your demands on performance according to the dog's breed or type, size, age, health and physical and mental fitness. It is rarely a problem to find a suitable dog as long as your personal skills as a trainer are good (being systematic, patient, etc.). The training methods I am about to describe are free of pain, discomfort and fear—totally harmless in other words—but effective.

Plan your training

The way the dog solves a task the first time will be the way she will try it again later in life when she meets up with a similar situation. This is true no matter how many months or years of training have passed between the events. So it is the very first track, the first search for hashish, the first search for a lost person, the first mushroom search, which is the most important in the dog's life! Therefore, do not go into training without having thought carefully through what you want to achieve. If you have not planned the training thoroughly, it is better to delay the training for later and just go for a nice walk.

How do dogs learn?

Dogs learn by association. Association means to connect one event with another. We associate, too. When I see a travel brochure, I immediately start to dream of travels I have enjoyed or someplace I would like to visit. Seeing someone grabbing their car keys, I assume they are about to leave. Dogs associate in the same way. Many dogs easily learn the difference between an office coat and a leisure coat. Your dog has learned to associate being taken for a walk whenever you put on a certain coat. Many dogs have learned the meaning of certain words without us even trying to teach them. Did you actually have to teach your dog the words "go for a walk" or "food?"

When teaching a dog a new behavior, I am conscious about when I apply a cue (the word I use to ask the dog to do a behavior). For example, when teaching Sit, I hold a treat over the dog's nose, and only when the dog sits will she get the treat. After a couple of repetitions, the dog will associate a treat above her nose with sitting. I will never tell the dog to "Sit" at this early stage. Only when your dog does what you want her to consistently should you "baptize" the behavior by giving it a name.

In my way of training, it is important that the dog only receives positive associations. I want my dog to work with me because *she* wants to. Force or punishment is something I never apply. However, I sometimes will remove the dog's chance to be reinforced, i.e., take away something the dog wants (negative punishment), if the dog does not perform. I will give the dog something she likes (positive reinforcement) to pay for good behavior.

The word "No," or other negative reactions to your dog's behavior, can be counter-effective during training, whether it be obedience, searching for bombs or agility training. When you say "No," jerk on the leash or do anything else to punish the dog, this will upset your dog. Because of the way the brain and nervous system work, negative feelings are learned stronger and faster than positive ones, so it does not help much to praise the dog for doing the right thing immediately after the correction. The negative impact has already been experienced.

Motivation

To ensure that your dog is willing to work for you at any time, it is crucial that she has sufficient motivation to do exactly what you want. The needed amount of motivation is achieved through providing her with the right reinforcement at the right time. Learning how to do this is not always easy, whether the reinforcement is positive or negative. Aristotle said, "Anybody can become angry, that is easy. But to be angry with the right person, and to the right degree, at the right time, for the right purpose and in the right way, that is not within everybody's power and is not easy."

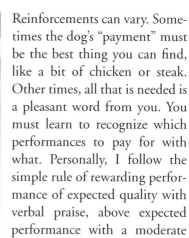

Reinforcements can vary. Sometimes the dog's "payment" must be the best thing you can find, like a bit of chicken or steak. Other times, all that is needed is a pleasant word from you. You must learn to recognize which performances to pay for with what. Personally, I follow the simple rule of rewarding performance of expected quality with verbal praise, above expected performance with a moderate value reward, and a great performance with the highest value reward (tailored to that dog's preferences).

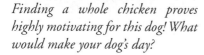

Finding a whole chicken proves highly motivating for this dog! What would make your dog's day?

Remember to pay attention to your own motivation as well. If you want progress in the training, both you and the dog must receive rewards that are worth the effort!

Food as reward/reinforcement

Food is my reward of preference, especially when teaching something new. We know that good effort will be given by any adult wild predators (or its domestic descendents) who are driven to seek out food for survival.

Treats for training must be small, fresh and juicy in order to function as quick and effective reinforcements. You should avoid using foods like biscuits that crumble easily or the dog may end up searching the ground for more goodies while you wait for her to be ready to continue training. You also don't want a situation where you "pay" with a ball and then the dog runs off to play with the ball—leaving you behind. Reinforcement with objects (toys) often takes too long for *initial* learning, and moves focus from the training to play. Additionally, toys can end up being a "negative" if you have to take the object from the dog either by force or by command.

A toy can be a great reward, but have a plan for getting it back!

The seven wonders of the (treat) world

Do you *really* know what your dog likes the best? I remember a story about training a polar bear. Imagine being in that situation. What would you use as treats? Fish, meat, fat? Good thinking, but not this time. This polar bear's favorite treat was raisins (Pryor, 2002). A Labrador retriever I met preferred cucumber. But most dogs prefer something from the butcher or, alternatively, fish or cheese.

Here is a way to find out what treats your dog likes best so you can reward her accordingly. Make a list ranking what your dog likes the most and then collect the things you want to test. Take a small piece of liver, for example, in one hand, and chicken in the other. Close your hands and then let the dog sniff to find out what you have. Then, hold your hands a little apart from each other. The hand your dog shows the most interest in will indicate the better of the two for your dog. Maybe chicken won over liver. Register the result, and carry on comparing chicken to all the other things—fish cakes, cheese, hot dog, waffle, whatever. Compare each thing with all the others, until you have a ranked list of your dog's "seven wonders of the world." This list will be your tool to help to pick the right payment in different situations. When your dog's motivation appears very low, surprise her by using a high ranking treat. Likewise, if the dog's performance has been very good, pick a high ranking treat. If the performance is OK, but not special, pick a treat from the bottom of the list.

Variable reinforcement

In addition to varying the treats, I use variable (intermittent) reinforcement. Variable reinforcement means simply that the dog never knows beforehand whether she will receive a treat. The idea is that your dog initially gets a treat every time until she starts to understand what you want. Normally that takes about three to six times. Then, you give a treat once every other time the dog gets it right for another three to six times. When the dog is getting very reliable (80% correct performance), you can start giving a treat around 25% to 35% of the time. That is variable reinforcement. You then continue with variable reinforcement for that learned behavior. Of course, you can praise every time, but be stingier with the treats. The point is that the dog should not know when a treat will come, or what will come. This actually will help you keep up your dog's excitement for the work. Think of yourself as a slot machine which sometimes gives money back, and sometimes not, instead of a vending machine which always gives a reward.

Jackpots

A jackpot is meant to be a very special reward for your dog. The jackpot's magic is to be given seldom and only for special efforts, so it doesn't lose its impact. Each time your dog performs extraordinarily well, give her a jackpot—an especially large or tasty treat or something else your dog prizes highly. The easiest way to do this is to have treats in sufficient amounts for five to six repetitions in your hand/pocket. When the dog has a breakthrough, I give what I have left in my hand as the jackpot. Jackpots may also be something totally different. If you train using food as reinforcement, a toy may be the jackpot. Freedom to do something of the dog's own choice may be a good jackpot. For Tan, a mine detection dog I trained, the best jackpot he could have was to play in water.

Once one of my dogs came when called (unexpectedly!) while chasing a cat. I had neither a toy nor a treat and did not really know how to pay my dog for this wonderful behavior. At the last minute,

I realized that I always have myself, so I improvised and acted like a clown by throwing myself on the ground, turning somersaults in the heather, laughing, playing and petting her. And guess what—it worked! You may be inventive in creating good reinforcements, but don't forget your own voice and body. After all, your voice and presence are always available!

A jackpot might include being allowed to romp in a stream.

Shaping and clicker training

As you will see from the descriptions of my training advice, my methods are very similar to shaping and clicker training. My personal experience is that clicker training may be well suited for training things like scent discrimination and other forms of nosework. If your dog is clicker trained, by all means you can use the clicker for many of the exercises I describe in the book.

Repetitions

Before you start, bear in mind the importance of not overdoing your training. Never ask your dog to repeat a behavior too many times in a row. Again, I have a golden rule for training new behaviors: do a maximum of five repetitions and then take a short break before attempting another one to five repetitions. Stop when the dog has done something well. The short break may only need to be about a minute.

If you have made five attempts at a behavior without any success, thank the dog for being so patient with you, and then figure out what went wrong. Was there too much in the way of distractions, was the dog ill, newly fed or very tired, were you grumpy, or was it simply too difficult for the dog for some reason?

If your dog performed perfectly on a first attempt, give a high value treat and take a short break. Always end the training session with the best you can expect. This establishes a positive learning atmosphere, leading to a dog who will look forward to future training sessions with joy. Whenever you have completed three to five sessions (one session consists of one to five repetitions), you need to take a longer break of ten minutes or more. In some cases, you may take a break for hours or days, depending on what you train. The duration and frequency of the break must be adjusted according to the dog in question and when she starts to be tired. Ideally, you should stop before her interest begins to sink. Remember, *setting the dog up for success is your responsibility.*

When do I go to the next step?
Another one of my golden rules is to move on to the next behavior when you have achieved 80% reliability on the behavior you have been teaching. A long time ago, I was taught to do at least eighty repetitions of a behavior before moving on. Luckily, we know better by now: it's the percentage rather than the total number of times your dog gets it right that counts. The dogs must have been frustrated or bored with such slow progress!

For some adult dogs, particularly adult females who are fast learners, you don't need to do even four or five repetitions to get a learned behavior that is reliable. I have seen dogs that "get it" after the first or second attempt. These dogs easily lose interest if you continue to ask them to do the same thing over and over. By moving to a new behavior or making an existing one more challenging (called "raising the criteria"), a dog's interest will perk up again.

Why taking breaks is beneficial to training

It may seem paradoxical that a book on dog training emphasizes taking breaks. I recommend them because I have learned that one of the most important tools in dog training is taking breaks. What to do with your dog in the break, the duration of the break, and when to take a break are all important questions.

Dogs taking a well deserved break from training.

A break allows both you and your dog a chance to rest, relax, digest what has been learned and to get ready for doing more afterwards. It is important that you know what is and is not relaxing for your dog. Each dog is different. Many dogs enjoy a nice rest in the car. Others will be hysterical about being left alone in the car, or they feel that it is their duty to guard the car and thus will be in work mode all the time and not rest at all.

In my classes, I often see owners use the breaks to train something else, like obedience, tricks, agility obstacles or whatever. This is normally a bad idea. When you train something else during a break, you take away the memory of what you (and the dog) just did, and replace it with what you are doing now. Additionally, the act of being trained is not a break anyway!

Playing with other dogs or running freely around during a break from training is also normally not a good idea, either. This also changes a dog's focus and is not really relaxing.

Nosework Tips
The most frequent reason for problems in the training is progressing too fast. On the other hand, the second reason for problems is prograssing too slowly. Find a balance of progression for you and your dog and you will avoid unnecessary frustrations. Take a few breaks and you will have a lot more fun!

I recommend that on a break you should just stroll around with the dog on leash, letting her sniff where she wants. If the training has been very long with a lot of thinking and difficult tasks involved, a little slow jogging may be good. On the other hand, if the training was very active with a lot of speed and action, a calm stroll or some sleep in the car may be good. Do not go directly from heavy activity to rest. Remember to cool the dog down first with a few minutes of slow walking. Learn from horse experts: warm up first and cool down afterwards!

Take breaks often and before you think they might be necessary. You can take a break in the midst of group training, provided that both you and your dog remember the session as positive. It may be that your dog performs very well on the very first try. Fine. Praise and treat and take a short break before carrying on with the same task. A short break may be only twenty seconds, or it may be more. We humans tend to think, "Wow, we have progress. This is fun. Let us do it one more time" and then, of course, it goes wrong. Stop in time! If the dog's interest (or yours) has begun to wane, you should take a break. The more you train, the more you will learn to see when it is time to take a break.

CHAPTER 4

Search for Treats

Exercise description. This is an exercise or game for your dog to do together with children or adults, indoors or outdoors, in the garden or in the fields or woods. The purpose is to have your dog search for and find hidden treats, some small and some large. Don't you think this is possible for you and your dog? After reading these few pages, you will see that it is not as complicated as you may think.

Goal. Your dog, searching all alone and without having seen you hide the treats, is able to sniff them all out.

Dogs are naturally made to use their noses, brains and legs in combination to search for food or anything else they want. We can take advantage of this drive in search work competitions or search and rescue tasks. In this exercise, we make it very elementary by letting the dog search for something that makes her really happy to find, and allows the dog to receive the reward on the spot.

All dog owners I have spoken to find this game easy and fun for both dogs and humans. Most dogs find great satisfaction in searching and finding food, and a dog that is good at this may search a huge area to find many tiny edible surprises. You will see how calm and content your dog becomes after this work. A session of goodie searching is far more stimulating than jogging or obedience training. After doing this exercise, your dog will be happy, content and ready for some rest.

This exercise will help your dog learn to search with great eagerness and thoroughness and is a great way to build a foundation for more complex search exercises like the "Square Search" which will be covered later. One advantage to using many small treats is that if the dog does not find them all, you can leave the treats for the ants or mice (if you are outside)!

Search for treats step by step

1. When beginning this exercise for the first time, hold your dog on leash regardless of whether you are indoors or outdoors. Make sure your dog is not given cues like "Sit," "Down" or "Wait." Simply hold onto the leash. Place yourself and the dog so that the dog is looking in the same direction as you, then throw a couple of treats no further than three to four feet away with the dog watching what you are doing. Once the treats land, let the dog run to find them. Join the party by praising your dog and telling her how wonderful a search dog she is. As the last treat is swallowed, call your dog back.

2. Remember, dogs learn faster than you think, so you should be prepared to increase the challenge very soon. Now, toss two or three treats immediately following each other, one at a time. Make sure the dog is watching and that the treats land pretty close to each other. Without any cue, let the dog run out and eat the treats. Join the party when the dog finds the goodies. If she finds only one, call her back and toss a few new ones in the same area. This way the missing treats will become bonuses in a later search. The more treats she finds, the more fun she will find this game. Repeat this step one or two times.

3. Now toss four or five treats, increasing both the distance you toss them and the distance between the treats. Your dog is probably beginning to get the hang of this game now. Continue to release your dog without giving any cue. Repeat this step two or three times.

4. Now is the time to introduce a cue. I like to use "Get your treats" or you can choose something else. This time toss two or three treats only. Say the cue right before you release the dog to go search. If your dog immediately goes out and searches successfully, repeat again with the cue, and continue to give the cue going forward. After a few repetitions, she will associate the cue with this game. If not, go back to Step 3.

If you have gone straight through the first four steps, you need to give your dog a major break now. Have it last a minimum of ten minutes, allowing her to sniff, walk, have water and rest. If she still appears tired, make the break really long, letting her sleep, and maybe even wait until tomorrow before continuing on. Start again at Step 4.

5. Toss even more treats, maybe eight to ten. Continue to throw them farther away from you and with greater distance between them. Give the cue "Get your treats" at the same time as you release the dog. Repeat one or two times.

6. Now it is time to increase the size of the search area and instead of throwing the treats you will walk around without the dog and drop them here and there. If your dog knows your Sit and Stay cues, she can sit and watch you while you hide the treats. If not, tie her to something, or have someone else help you by holding your dog. If your dog finds this very stressful, you should hold her while someone else walks around placing the treats. Hide many treats, at least ten, and spread them widely around the area. The area may be as big as 100 square yards or even bigger if your dog is long legged.

At this point, it is time for a major break. The dog should totally relax without doing anything. The break should last at least thirty minutes. If your break lasts over night, begin one to three step(s) behind the level where you stopped. Otherwise, move on to Step 7.

7. Now you are going to prevent your dog from seeing you hide the treats, a significant increase in the difficulty of

the task. Have the dog wait indoors, in another room, or in a covered crate while you place some treats in the area. Since she doesn't see you hide the treats this time, try to make it easier for her to find them the first time you do this. Instead of spreading them widely, place the treats where you expect she can find them easily and quickly. Get your dog, hold her like you have done before, give the cue "Get your treats" and release her. If she starts searching now, you know she learned the cue, and you have reached your goal. Congratulations! If she fails this step, no harm done. Go back to Step 6 two or three times before trying Step 7 again.

8. Now increase the size of the search area even more to a level appropriate for your dog. Consider the size of your dog, her speed and how fast she works. It should be no problem for a fit Labrador or Setter to search an area the size of a football field. Most people will be satisfied with a smaller area, though. A meadow may be the perfect spot, or a calm corner in a nearby park.

You may vary how long the treats are laying there before the search begins. Sometimes it is easier to find "old" treats, sometimes not. Play and experiment finding out what your dog can cope with. Make it a game between you and the dog, or between the kids and the dog. The point of the game is to hide the treats, making it a real challenge finding them. Repeat at least once per week for the rest of your dog's life.

9. Generalize the search. This means you should see if your dog can learn to search for treats in all types of environments, indoors or outdoors. If the training started in a particular room, expand now so your dog will search through more and more rooms, maybe in other houses, and also in the garden and/or the park or woods. Vary the type of woods, type of meadow, height of grass, type of vegetation, etc. Do this exercise in any possible and "impossible" places.

Keep in mind

In the beginning of this exercise, you must always make sure to take a break or finish when your dog still wants more. If you carry on until the dog gets tired, she may lose interest for this exercise. Especially in the beginning while she is concentrating hard, it is crucial to remember this. Later, when the dog knows the game and likes it very much, you can let her work until she stops on her own.

During the initial training of this game, my recommendation is that you choose the same location to work in for an entire session, whether indoors or outdoors. This is so that if the dog does not find all the treats in a search, they remain there as a bonus for the following searches. Your dog receives more reinforcement, and may even learn the game faster.

If your dog, for any reason, does not find the hidden treats, do not show her where they are. Let them stay where they are, and after the training is over you can either remove them or leave them for other animals.

The little Dachshund in Japan

I would like to share with you the story about how this little Dachshund learned to use her nose. In Japan, most small dogs are pets in the broadest sense of the word. So was the case for this little one. She was an adult, but had no experience in using her nose for anything. We set up an exercise where the treats were placed on the ground six to ten feet from her. The dog was watching all the time. When she was supposed to start searching, she remained standing and sniffing around her own legs. Not until we cut the distance down to about two feet did she get the idea that she was supposed to sniff out the treats. But then she really got it, and searched very thoroughly and eagerly. She found all the tiny treats underneath the dead leaves, and chewed them happily. During the first couple of training sessions, we were able to more than double the size of the search area!

CHAPTER 5

Hide and Seek

Exercise description. "Hide and Seek" is very similar to the "Search for Treats," exercise covered in the last chapter. The major difference is that the dog is asked to find objects, not food. Dogs who enjoy carrying things in their mouths should find this game just as fun as finding treats. You will need a toy or something else that your dog loves and which she enjoys holding in her mouth. Personally, I would play this game inside a house or a fenced yard to avoid having the dog not wanting to come back to me with her treasure. An important difference in this exercise is that if your dog does not find the hidden object (and it is something you don't want to lose), you will have to remember where it is hidden and pick it up yourself! This game is also suitable for the kids to play with the dog.

Goal. Your dog will search for and find an object or favorite toy. It does not really matter whether or not the dog returns to you with the toy—the point is only to search for it and find it by using her nose. Maybe you remember the game of Hide and Seek from your childhood? This is not difficult to teach your dog.

Hide and Seek step by step

1. Throw a toy in front of the dog while she is watching, then let her run and find it right away. Do not use a cue. Share the joy when your dog finds it. If your dog brings

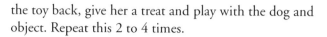

the toy back, give her a treat and play with the dog and object. Repeat this 2 to 4 times.

2. Most dogs learn faster than we believe, so now you will make things a bit more challenging. This time, throw the toy a little farther, maybe even so it lands hidden behind something, out of sight of the dog. However, make sure that the dog knows roughly where it ended up. Once the toy has landed, release the dog to run forward for the toy, still without giving any cue. Like before, share the dog's joy with praise when she finds the object. Repeat 2 to 3 times.

This is a good time to give your dog a break of a few minutes. After the break, warm up with Step 2 again before continuing on to Step 3.

3. Give a cue or hand signal for Sit/Stay and go just beyond the reach of your dog's vision before you lay down the object. If she does not know Sit/Stay, tether her or have someone hold her for you. Return immediately to the dog, then let her run out to find the object. If you are training inside, you may have your dog wait in a room and close the door. Repeat this 1 to 3 times.

4. Now it is time to increase the size of the search area. Again, use Sit/Stay, a tether or a helper. Go to where the dog cannot see you and hide the object without making it too difficult. Walk around a little after laying down the object to avoid the dog being able to follow your scent path to where you hid the toy. Repeat this 2 to 5 times.

5. Now you should teach your dog a cue for this game. Say "Hide-and-seek" or something else of your choice at the same moment you release your dog to search for the object. You want to make sure that you are convinced your dog will start to search once released before you add the cue. Be careful not to give the cue unless you are quite sure the dog will get it right. Repeat this step 2 to 5 times.

Time for a break again. Let the dog totally relax and do little or nothing. Go for a little walk, relax indoors, whatever. If you stop here for the day, when you start up again, go back to Step 3, just to see what the dog remembers. Then, go quickly through Steps 4-5 again before you go to Step 6.

6. Now, do not allow your dog to see you hide the toy. Have the dog wait in another room or in a covered crate, depending on where you are. Hide one of her favorite toys, but choose a location that is not too difficult, since you do not want her to give up before finding it. Get the dog, give your "Hide-and-seek" cue, and let her go. If she starts searching now, you know she learned the cue, and you have reached your goal. Congratulations! If she fails this step, go back to Step 5 two or three times before trying Step 6 again. No harm done.

7. Now increase the size of the search once again to make the exercise more difficult. If you are doing this indoors, hide the toys behind furniture, under carpets, on a shelf, between the cushions—use your imagination. If you are outdoors, continue to expand the size of the search area gradually until it is about the size of a football field, especially if you have a large dog.

8. The last step is to vary how long the toy is hidden before you release your dog to search for it. Sometimes it is easier to find objects that have been hidden for a while. Vary the time and experiment to see how it impacts your dog's ability to find the toy. And finally, let your kids hide the toy: this should be a game that gives both kids and dogs a great playtime together.

This is what you want to see—a dog highly motivated to get the hidden toy!

Keep in mind

When training this exercise, make sure to stop when your dog still wants more! If you carry on until the dog gets tired, she may lose interest. You want to avoid that happening, especially in the beginning steps when the real learning begins. Later, when the dog knows the game and likes it, too, you may let her work until she gives up sometimes.

For some dogs, you may find that they are only willing to search for one particular toy. For other dogs, you may have to change toys or objects frequently to keep them motivated.

A fun variation

You may have noticed something missing in the Hide and Seek game, at least based on how I used to play it as a kid. We used to call out "Hotter" when the searcher got nearer to the object, and

"Colder" when the searcher moved away from the hiding place. You can also do this with dogs. She will intensify her search when hearing the word "Hotter" if you always say it when she gets close to the object. I recommend, however, that you take the dog through all the steps first—to make sure she masters the exercise—before adding this variation.

Dirham and the purse...

Many years ago I had a Belgian Tervueren who was certified by the Norwegian Association of Search & Rescue Dogs. He enjoyed finding things that people had "lost," which he was trained to do on my signal. Once, as we walked through my town, he insisted on investigating a tight shrubbery by the footpath. I could trust him, so I let him loose. After rummaging through the shrubbery for a short while, he ducked out with a purse between his jaws, and something like a big smile on his face. The purse no longer contained any money, but did contain some personal property. I gave it to the police. The day after, I was informed that the purse belonged to an old lady who had been robbed some days before. She was very happy to get it back since it contained her old Bible.

CHAPTER 6

Naming Your Dog's Toys

Exercise description. This is a fun variation of the Hide and Seek exercise from the previous chapter. Somewhere in the house, the garden or the woods lies "Teddy." ("Teddy" can be any kind of toy.) You will ask your dog to go and find Teddy, passing by any other toys along the way. In this game, it is only Teddy that counts, nothing else. Teddy has either been hidden by you, or it just remains where it was left after it was played with last. You will want to choose a toy or something else of your dog's preference and then use it through all the initial training.

Goal. Your dog will search for and find a specific named toy or object, ignoring other objects.

Naming your dog's toys step by step

1. Hold Teddy in front of your dog, then invite your dog to take it using as little movement as possible. Once she grabs it, say "Teddy" in a nice and encouraging way, then praise and play as reward. Repeat this 2 to 5 times.

2. Instead of holding Teddy in your hand, place Teddy on the floor in front of the dog. If the dog does not take it by herself, invite the dog to grab Teddy by playing "keep away" with Teddy and the dog. At the moment when

the dog grabs Teddy, say "Teddy" and praise and play again. Repeat this 1 to 5 times in a row.

3. Now we will begin to slightly increase the difficulty. Hold the dog gently by the harness, and place Teddy on the floor out of her reach, making sure she can see Teddy. Now release her and once she starts to move toward Teddy, say the word "Teddy." After repeating this two to five times, it is likely your dog has learned to understood the cue.

If you trained all three of these steps in a row, you should take a break of at least ten minutes. After the break, start with something slightly easier than what you ended up with to warm up. You are ready for Step 4 once your dog consistently moves toward the toy on your cue of "Teddy."

4. Now is the time to start placing Teddy out of sight of your dog. Show Teddy to her (she is either on a Sit/Stay, tethered or being held by someone), then hide Teddy behind a doorway or a piece of furniture, making sure she cannot see it from where she is. Go back to her, let her go and praise her a lot when she finds Teddy. I do not recommend giving the cue the first time you hide Teddy out of sight. Regard this first hiding as a test and, if it works well, repeat, then add the cue the moment you release the dog. Repeat 1 to 5 times.

5. Now we will increase the difficulty so that Teddy is not visible when hidden. You want your dog to really have to use her nose to find Teddy under a cushion or behind a piece of furniture. But don't make it so difficult that she will give up. The level of difficulty must only be increased gradually. If it was too difficult for your dog, make it easier to find Teddy, praise a lot and take a break. Never ever be tempted to help your dog to solve the problem. If you do, you only teach her that it pays to give up. Repeat 1 to 5 times.

6. Now test to see that your dog understands the difference between Teddy and the other toys. Place Teddy with one or two other toys all visible on the floor, with Teddy closest to your dog. Say "Teddy," and let the dog loose to work by herself. If she chooses correctly, you have reached your goal. Congratulations! If she picks the wrong toy, ignore this, go back to Step 3 and work forward through the steps once more. Whenever your dog touches one of the other toys, look the other way, and do not accept it if she wants to give it to you. Hopefully, she will then leave this toy and go back to searching. When she now picks Teddy, make it a birthday and Christmas celebration at the same time! Give a jackpot, and take a break. Repeat this step, varying the position of Teddy between the others, until your dog reliably picks Teddy and ignores anything else. But again—do only one to five repetitions in a row.

7. Now that your dog knows Teddy's name, start to hide more toys in the house, including Teddy, in gradually more difficult-to-find places. Ask your dog to find Teddy, making a big party whenever she finds it. Any mistakes? Return to Step 6.

8. If you wish to take this trick even further, take Teddy and the other toys into other locations such as your garden, the park, the woods, a meadow or a friend's place. Go through all the steps from the beginning in each new location.

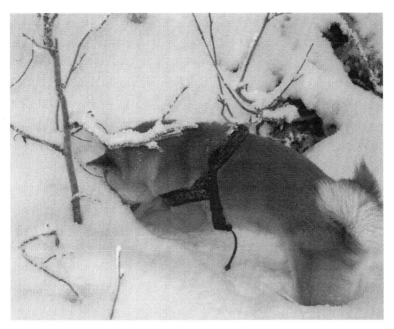

Hide the toy in increasingly difficult places.

9. Once your dog has obviously learned which toy Teddy is, teach her the name of other toys, one-by-one, following the same recipe. Pick names of toys that *sound* different, not only ones that have a different meaning.

Keep in mind

It may be difficult for your dog to ignore Teddy in the beginning of teaching the name of other new toys (Step 6). Use "neutral" or "cold" toys first (toys that do not yet have a name and that are not as interesting to your dog). When the new name is fully learned, you can start to teach the difference between "Teddy" and "Ball," for example. Just do a couple repetitions and stop before your dog gets confused. Very often one repetition is enough at this stage!

Another method of teaching your dog the name of toys is to simply just wait until she bites a toy. At the very same moment she grabs the toy, say the name and praise and play with it. After some repetitions, she will learn the names of the toys ("Ball," "Teddy," "The Red One," etc.) this way.

Say the name of the toy as your dog bites it, then offer play as a reward.

Another great trick is to teach your dog a name of your slippers. Imagine having a dog that gets your slippers when asked!

> ### Head = brains over legs!
> On a workshop in Germany in autumn 2003, my students reported on a dog who had recently been on German TV. He was a young Border Collie who had been injured and had to be kept calm for a few months. Not a very easy task! His owners found a way: they trained the dog to use his brain instead of his legs. Dogs get just as tired from thinking as from running. This young Border Collie learned the name of all his toys and many others, and eventually he knew the name of roughly 200 toys!

CHAPTER 7

The Square Search

Exercise description. Square Searching is a way of teaching your dog the art of searching for things that we humans have lost. Once learned, this can evolve into a competitive sport or a deadly serious endeavour with lives at stake. However, for most dogs and their owners, it is solely for amusement.

Your dog sniffs along the ground, in paths forward and back from where you are standing. She runs and works eagerly, moving out 50 to 60 yards away from you and then making a turn coming directly back to you. After praise or a reward, you move laterally several steps sideways and send your dog out and back again in a similar fashion.

The search will normally end when the dog scents something, picks it up (assuming the item is small enough), and then comes rushing back to you. Perhaps she is holding a small piece of cloth, a match box car or a leather glove. She has already learned that you get very happy for such things. Just as happy as she gets for the chicken neck you pay her with!

Goal. At your direction, your dog will make a thorough search of an area by completing a series of 150 foot long search paths.

Many people think I am too much of a control freak, because I want to direct where in the field the dog is searching. Maybe they are right. I got into this habit during the years of training dogs to find

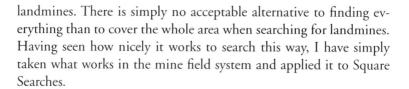

landmines. There is simply no acceptable alternative to finding everything than to cover the whole area when searching for landmines. Having seen how nicely it works to search this way, I have simply taken what works in the mine field system and applied it to Square Searches.

Square Searches step by step

Before you begin, you will need some very good treats, an object your dog loves dearly and a helper. Take everything with you to a peaceful field, meadow or other quiet place to begin training. Your dog should already know how to retrieve (see Chapter 9 if need be). I also recommend using treats rather than play to get the dog to exchange whatever she finds, as playing removes focus from what we are actually training. Once the dog is more experienced in the game, I start to play with the objects as a variation (or addition) to the treats.

1. This first step will focus on building your dog's desire to work. You want both the item she is to find and the treat you use to get her to exchange the found item to be things she likes. Start off by tying your dog to a tree or hold her on leash. Then you (or your helper) will create a scent trail by walking about 15 to 25 yards, then zig-zagging back side-to-side within a 3 to 4 yard wide trail. Make sure your dog sees what you or the helper intends to hide. Drop the glove or toy or whatever you have, and then zig-zag your way back. What you have done is to create a scent trail which is meant to help your dog keep on track as she moves out toward the glove. The first few times you let the dog go for the glove, do it without giving any cue. When your dog finds the glove, praise, and when she returns to you with the object, then exchange it for that special treat. Be ready. Don't make the dog wait for the treat! Repeat this 1 to 5 times, using the same scent trail, before taking a break.

Walk away 15-25 yards from your dog and then drop the object. Zig-zag your way back to the dog.

2. Keep repeating Step 1, but begin to gradually increase the length of the scent trail in 5 to 10 yard increments. Most dogs will be able to handle the longer distance in just a few repetitions. What is important is that you always make it a *little* more difficult, trying to insure that the dog will have a fair chance for success. Understand that the feeling of mastering promotes learning. When your dog can consistently find the item you hide at a distance of 50 to 60 yards, it is time to introduce the cue for this game.

3. In this case, you have already established a visual cue for this exercise in the form of you or your helper going out and hiding an object. However, before I introduce the verbal cue, I want to make sure that the dog is successful at Steps 1 and 2. I do not wish to give the dog the cue for a Square Search only to watch her run to the creek for a dip. A clever dog might learn that the word "Square" means take a dip in one to two repetitions! Have your dog do two easy short searches with easy to find objects. If you are convinced that she will be perfect again, introduce the cue.

   At the moment you release the dog, say "Square" or something else of your choice. Exactly what you say is not really the point, but it must sound different from all other cues your dog has learned, and you must say it the same way each time. If successful, stop the exercise with a really good reward, play with the object and take a break. After a short break, send her out without a cue before giving the cue for a second search.

   Do 3 to 5 sessions of a couple repetitions each with the cue. That works well for most dogs. Then it is high time for a major break. As always, stop when the dog is being successful and still wants more.

4. You are still making a scent trail as before at this point. Now, however, your dog is no longer allowed to watch

you or your helper place the object. She should be positioned so she cannot see or hear what is going on.

In the same zigzag fashion, hide a favorite object. Remember that whenever making something more difficult, the other variables must be made easier if possible. So, keep the trail relatively short and make sure the object is not well hidden. You are really just testing whether the dog will search without having seen anyone hide anything and if your cue continues to work as before.

If the first search in this step goes well, give your dog a reward and take a short break. Then make a new scent path and try it again. If the dog is not successful, go back to Step 3 before trying Step 4 again.

5. This stage involves training your dog to Square Search without a scent path to help her. This may be the most critical step in the training. The key to this step is what I call "planned success," and the key to accomplishing it is to place the object at a location and distance where you know your dog will find it. If your dog always rushes out and starts to search ten yards away, place the object there. If she starts searching only three yards away, then place it there. You want her to learn that whenever you say "Square," there is something out there, even if the scent trail is missing. So make it easy in the beginning of this step.

Nosework Tips

Placing the object without creating a scent trail can be tricky. If you are good at throwing, the problem is solved. Otherwise, use your imagination, but just make sure there is not a scent trail leading to the object. You can also walk out parallel or on a curved pattern to where the search is to be conducted and then throw the object to where you want it to be.

Gradually place the object farther and farther way until the dog can reliably find it without a scent trail at a distance of 50 to 60 yards. If the object is placed too far away, she may start to search to the left or right before she gets to the object. If it is placed too close, the dog may run over it without noticing. If this happens, move out in the direction that your dog has gone off course and call her back to you. Ideally, she should be prevented from finding the object when she has run way off course! If she does find it anyway, you just have to praise/reward and make a new (and better) plan.

6. This step teaches your dog to begin searching right from her first step once given the cue to do so. I find that most dogs show a pattern of rushing out 10, 30 even 50 yards before nose and brain are connected. To make sure your dog will find everything efficiently, you want to teach her to be in "search mode" right from the very first step.

   If your dog's pattern is to rush out 20 yards before searching, then place the search object out 20 yards and pay your dog for finding it. Then, gradually reduce the distance—18 yards, 15 yards and so on—giving jackpots for significant progress. Carry on like this until your dog starts to search sooner, placing the object closer and closer to the starting line until she can find objects laying just a foot or two from your feet. Now you can be sure that your dog is searching from the very beginning!

   Once your dog is searching successfully near the starting point, vary where the object is placed. Always, however, remember to place the object within a 3 to 4 yard wide search path. I recommend working in high grass or heather and using a rather large object. If you have only short grass available, pick a smaller object of high value. Make sure the object is not visible, as your dog is supposed to sniff to find it.

7. Up until this step, there has been something within the search area for your dog to find even if she did not always find it. That means she has not been exposed to what I call an "empty search." Nevertheless, you must expose your dog to empty searches to make sure you can have confidence that she will continue working even when it takes a long time before she finds anything. To make sure your dog does not run sideways and find an object she was supposed to find later, you have to plan and prepare. One good idea is to place an object before working with your dog, using a path or tree as a landmark so you remember where it is. Then send your dog out searching in another direction where you know there is nothing to find. When the dog has reached a distance of 50 to 60 yards, call her back and praise her. Then send her out in the direction towards where the object is hidden and have a big party when she finds the object!

Another way you can do this is to use the wind to your advantage. Place an object down wind so that it cannot carry scent from the object to your starting point. To be absolutely sure, walk as far away from the object as necessary so your dog will not find it. Once again send her out, praise her while at an appropriate distance and call her back after she has searched. Then, orient yourself so that you are near the object and the wind will carry the scent toward where you and the dog started. Send her out searching and join the party when she finds the object. If she does not find it, send her out once again.

Each time your dog has searched somewhere where nothing was to be found, follow that with a series of trials of at least 4 to 5 times in a row where she will find an object. Then it is time to send her out on two new empty searches in a row. Praise her once she reaches the wanted distance, and call her back. On the third search she must be set up to find an object of particular value to her! Keep following the same strategy and gradually build up the number of empty searches until your dog can do at least 4 to 5 runs in a row without finding anything and without losing her motivation. Then, vary the ratio of empty searches with those where she finds something. Your dog should not be able to guess (or learn!) how many empty searches in a row there will be—she must always believe there is a good chance that there will be an object to find every time you say the cue "Square."

Generalizing the square search behavior

Now your goal should be to teach your dog to search on all types of ground, in all kinds of environments and in all kinds of weather—in others words you are generalizing the training. At this point, you have an almost fully trained Square Search dog! The only thing remaining is to build up the dog's experience and motivation in working in all types of terrain. Many owners have learned the hard way that their dogs do not perform well in competitions because they have not experienced working in a new type of landscape.

Square Searching in grass is quite different from working in heather, especially if the dog is only used to one or the other. So, you need to make an effort to vary the training area frequently. As soon as your dog masters one type of terrain, move to another type. Always lower your expectations of what she can do when you change environments. Regard it as a totally new training task, which is how your dog will regard it! The more new types of environments you work in, the faster she will start to generalize, and you should see her adjust to new environment more easily.

The weather is another factor that many dog handlers ignore. It is easy and tempting to skip training in bad weather. However, the result of not being trained in bad weather is that either your dog may not be able to cope with it at all or she will perform poorer than normal when exposed to it. And we claim that it is the dog that dislikes the weather!

Many years ago I tried an experiment. At that time, I had a Belgian Tervuren who was a certified search and rescue dog in the Norwegian Association of Avalanche Dogs. Dirham was his name and he learned to love working in the rain. This is because I often took treats and toys and went out into the forest to train tracking or Square Searching when it rained. I did this consciously because I wanted to see which effect it had, and it worked. He became totally uninfluenced by bad weather his entire life, and in fact he became very motivated to train in rainy weather. Just try it yourself.

Keep in mind

High motivation or high stress? Many dogs become very excited, even stressed, by watching the helper run and hide the object. This is why my goal in training is to move away from motivating the dog that way as soon as possible. For some dogs it may be necessary to remove the visual cue even earlier than I have suggested. Anyway, you should always do only the minimum number necessary to catch the dog's attention. You want your dog to work fast but thoroughly with high concentration. If she gets stressed, she may move fast, but will not concentrate well and may have problems remembering what she actually is supposed to search for while running. Far too many mistakes happen when high stress is misinterpreted to be high motivation.

Trouble with giving back objects. Some dogs struggle with giving the objects back to their owners in a nice and calm fashion. Remember that this is a detail you train separately (at home, at a training club) before you start training the Square Search. Vary the objects you use—big, small, heavy, light, hard, soft—some are more enjoyable for the dog than others. Make sure that the payment the dog gets is always worth as much or more than the object she gives you! Before starting a Square Search exercise, it can even be a good idea to warm up with training giving back some objects.

Desire for objects. This is yet another thing you train before you begin the Square Search exercise. Remember, when you train the Square Search you only want to use objects you know your dog likes and will retrieve happily. Experiment beforehand with all kinds of objects in many locations like your house, a garden, a forest, etc. Place an object on the floor or ground, and when your dog shows interest, praise immediately. Maybe you will have to hold it in your hand initially before placing it on the floor, and then gradually increase the distance between dog and object while expecting more and more interest before you click/praise.

Build interest in the item you want your dog to find before attempting a new exercise.

The dog's dependency on helpers and the wind. If you motivate your dog by using a helper to hide objects for too long a period, you risk that she will become dependent on such support. Therefore, I recommend you test out how the training goes without a helper sometimes (tether the dog while you hide the object). If that does not work, then continue using a helper for a short while before trying it on your own again. In the case your dog succeed without a helper, then don't use one as you progress further.

Help from the wind is another means of support on which the dog may become dependent. Don't always place the object so the dog searches into the wind and the scent is easier to follow. During the training, I recommend that you frequently make little tests to see what she can do without such help. Use the wind only when you need extra motivation for your dog, but don't let her get dependent upon it.

When things go wrong. Whenever something goes wrong, sit down and think! What caused the "failure?" Make a new plan and do what you can to eliminate any reasons for mistakes.

Finished Square Searches and Competitions

When your dog is fully trained, I recommend that you frequently (but irregularly) conduct a complete Square Search with several hidden objects over a wide area as a test to see if your training has been successful. While you or a helper can hide the objects, it is even better if someone else hides the objects so that neither you nor your dog know where they are hidden. By doing this, you can see if your dog can cover the entire field, if she completes each phase of the search and if she can use the wind to her advantage. Allow your dog to search freely in the square if she chooses to. You can always call her and send her straight out if necessary so that you can cover every part of the search area. You will find that dogs have the ability to search systematically without us training them. With these two search systems (the dog searching on her own and the out and back scent path technique), you and your dog will cover a field efficiently. And you will see how pleased and content your dog will be after having searched and found things for you.

You can continue to do Square Searches just for fun, or you will now be in a position to start entering search competitions and even help take part in a search and rescue operation. Regard any competition as a test to see that your training system works and the cooperation between you and your dog works the way you want it to.

Tacu, the dog who rescued our training area

During my time as dog handler in the Norwegian Association of Avalanche Dogs, we had a little team of handlers who worked well together with several certified dogs. One of our most frequently used training areas was in a strip of woodland owned by the government. During the moose hunting season, a team of hunters were unhappy with us using the same area, even though we normally did not use the area at the same time they were hunting in it. While we did consider whether we should change training areas for a while, we were saved by one of the dogs. Tacu, a Rottweiler, was out searching one day and when he returned to his handler he was carrying a VHF radio in his mouth. He had apparently found it while searching for hidden persons, and chosen to bring it back to "Dad" since there might be a treat to earn! The radio was undamaged and fully functional. Tacu's handler figured it probably belonged to the hunters, so he searched for and found that the radio belong to them. (At this time, a radio like this would cost a month's salary.) After having gotten their radio back and learning one of our dogs had found it, they saw that it was a good thing that we still trained there!

CHAPTER 8

Finding Keys and Other Lost Items

What a great skill to teach a dog!

You are back at your car after a walk in the park. Both you and your dog are tired, but satisfied. When you go to unlock the car door, you realize that your keys are gone. It is already dusk, and of course it is too far to walk home. Now what? No problem—you just tell your dog to go find your keys. Three minutes later she returns with your keys in her mouth and a happy grin on her face. Great, isn't it?

Exercise description. This exercise involves teaching a dog to find a specific lost item, and then either return it to you or bark to indicate that she has found it. The dog pictured on the previous page took the keys in her mouth to return with them, while another dog could very well have found the keys and barked to get you to come and see what she found. Both solutions may be equally suitable and can be trained. Barking of course will be a better alternative if the item is too large to carry and for dogs who do not enjoy carrying things in their mouths. And, it is a nice way of telling you that the keys have been found. Your dog can learn this with no great effort—fully trained— and you can impress your friends that your dog is able to pick *your* car keys between any number of keys from the same spot.

Goal. To find a specific lost item and either bring it back to you or indicate that she has found it by barking.

This training exercise is broken into four phases, although it is still taught in a step-by-step format. I will use car keys as an example, but other items (wallet, cell phone) can be used equally well, not to mention that they are frequently lost!

Phase 1. Establish a strong interest for car keys in your dog.

1. Start by holding your keys in front of your dog. The same moment she sniffs them, praise and give a treat. Repeat 1 to 5 times, then take a short break.

2. Continue praise/clicking and treating for sniffing the keys, moving them gradually closer to the ground each time the dog sniffs them. Repeat 1 to 5 times.

3. Now place the keys on the ground (or floor, if you train indoors). Once your dog sniffs them, praise/click and toss a treat to the dog in such a way that will make her move away from the keys. This is an important mo-ment—wait and see if your dog returns to the keys by

herself. Say nothing, just wait. When she comes back to the keys the first time on her own, give her a jackpot and take a break. If your dog shows no more interest in the keys, stop the training and take a break. Start again at Step 1 and repeat all the steps. If she still does not return to the keys, you may need to change to better treats. Repeat this step until your dog happily runs (or walks) to the keys.

Repeat this first phase until your dog easily goes to your keys when you place them on the floor or ground. If your dog makes a mistake, give her another chance to get it right. Make sure you always stop with something successful. It is better to stop the training too early than too late. You can never make too few repetitions, you can easily make too many....

Phase 2. This phase deals with what the dog should do when she finds your keys. You need to decide if you want her to retrieve them, mark them with her paw, or if you want her to bark until you come and see what she has found. You may either decide this yourself, or wait and see what your dog prefers. Many dogs start to retrieve by themselves during this phase of the training.

1. At this stage, start to delay your praise/click while your dog sniffs the keys. First, wait maybe a half second, then longer and longer. Watch if your dog does something else to make you react with a treat. Some will start to paw the keys. If you are happy with this, reward when your dog does it. Repeat a maximum of five times. When your dog offers a sniff or pawing that you find satisfying, go to the next phase (Phase 3). If you want her to retrieve, go to step 2.

2. Do you wish your dog to retrieve the lost item? If so, you should withhold your praise longer and longer, just let the dog play vigorously with the keys, using her paws or whatever. Watch carefully, then whenever she has her mouth close to the keys, praise/click and treat. Gradually the idea that it is the snout and not the paw that counts will pop into her mind.

3. Continue watching the dog's mouth. If she opens her mouth in the vicinity of the keys, give a jackpot! Some dogs do this more readily than others. Are you lucky enough that your dog just picks the keys up by herself? If so, you have achieved your goal and should go to the next phase. If not, carry on delaying the praise and remain patient. Repeat in sessions of 1 to 5 repetitions until your dog grabs and lifts the keys.

What can happen here is that the dog's frustration grows if you do not praise as you did before. When her frustration increases, so does her activity level. However, if you wait too long, the dog will lose her interest entirely and may just walk away from the whole key project. The balance you are trying to maintain between keeping up her interest and withholding praise hoping to get some more progress is both difficult and important. If your dog loses her interest in the keys, go back to the very beginning (Phase 1) and through all the steps and phases once again. No harm done: it only takes some more time.

Phase 3. This phase is aimed at teaching your dog that it is only *your* keys that count, and no one else's. Now you need someone to help you. As you train your dog to sort out only *your* keys, do not touch any other keys you need to use in this phase. Once you touch other keys, they will contain your scent and the difference between your keys and the others will not be so clear to the dog.

1. Place your keys and have your helper place her keys on the ground 2 or 3 feet apart and so the dog can see both sets of keys. Place the keys so that your dog will come to your keys first. Be quick to praise for sniffing your keys, before she has time to leave them and go sniffing the other keys. If your dog chooses the wrong keys, ignore her and try again in a way so the chance of that happening again is reduced. If you still have no success, go back to Phase 2. Repeat 1 to 5 times and, as always, stop with the best you can expect.

2. Fairly soon, start to vary the position of the two sets of keys. Place them right next to each other as a next step, and then make it harder by placing your keys so that your dog must pass the "wrong" keys to get to them. Do not cheat. You must always change the position of the keys to avoid the dog from just rushing to them without sniffing. Remember not to touch the other keys. Repeat this until your dog easily picks out your keys and ignores the other ones.

3. Now repeat Step 2. However, this time use three sets of keys. One set is yours and the other two belong to your friends or training mates. Continue to ignore any mistakes and praise/click then treat or play when your dog makes the right choice. Repeat until she easily picks your keys from the three different key rings.

4. Gradually increase the number of keys to choose between. You may notice that six sets of keys are no more difficult than three. What may be difficult is whether your dog can pick your keys from the keys of others in your family.

5. When a larger number of keys is no longer difficult, vary the distance between the different keys. Try having them gradually closer until they all lay in one pile and your dog has to dig through them all to find yours!

6. Add a cue ("Keys," for example) for this behavior when your dog is consistently successful in finding and picking out your keys.

Phase 4. Involves a real search in addition to picking out the right keys.

1. Now you will begin to hide the keys so that your dog must search for them. The first time, have two sets of keys hidden (or maybe just one to make it easier). The keys should be within two feet of each other, and make sure they cannot be seen by the dog. Give your dog the

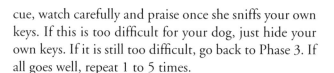

cue, watch carefully and praise once she sniffs your own keys. If this is too difficult for your dog, just hide your own keys. If it is still too difficult, go back to Phase 3. If all goes well, repeat 1 to 5 times.

2. Now increase the distance between the keys. Place them out of sight of the dog, though still close enough for you to watch what is going on. Allow the dog to search without interrupting her. If she chooses the wrong keys, go back to Phase 3. Praise whenever she reacts to your own keys. Repeat this until your dog easily searches and finds your own keys, and retrieves them or marks them according to the training done in Phase 2.

3. As soon as searching and marking/retrieving work well with two sets of keys, increase step-by-step the number of keys hidden in the terrain or in the room.

4. The last challenge is to increase the distance from the starting point out to where the keys are hidden. Increase this gradually. In order for this to be a useful behavior, I recommend anywhere from 20 to 120 yards, depending on your lifestyle and how you wish to work with your dog.

Keep in mind

Be aware that you should only increase the difficulties one criterion at a time. Either you increase the distance to the keys, the number of keys or the spacing between all the keys. It may be more difficult for the dog when she has to pass many keys before finding the right ones. Out of sheer frustration, she may choose to retrieve the wrong keys just to find a solution. Watch that you always stop the training before your dog is tired or too excited, since that's when the chance for mistakes is greatest.

When training with key rings, be aware that their different appearance will also make a difference to the dog. Some people have big and flashy amulets attached to their keys, while others are quite sober. It may be a good idea to remove the biggest charms from the key rings to prevent your dog from solving the task using her vision. Don't forget that dogs always will solve a problem the easiest way! And don't limit this behavior to just keys. You don't want to lose your wallet or cell phone either!

Clever boy, Ajax!

Ajax the clever key dog with his owner Annika.

How often do we underestimate our dog's capabilities? Ajax, a Swedish Bouvier des Flanders, was supposed to learn the trick to finding Mom's keys, but had apparently got the hang of it long before the humans. He had quickly learned to go over to Mom's keys and bring them to her while ignoring anyone else's. However, Mom had a helper who also had keys and who Ajax decided he should help as well. Without being taught to do so, he began to resolutely get the "wrong" keys and go straight to the helper with them, then go back to Mom's keys, which he picked up and gave to her. So smart and well mannered!

CHAPTER 9

The Lost Retrieve

Imagine having a dog who is able to retrace your steps, whether it was in a forest or around your neighborhood, and can pick up and return to you what you have lost along your route. It is a very helpful skill and a great means of exercise and mental stimulation for your dog. And it is not difficult to learn, although your dog must have been taught how to retrieve prior to learning this behavior. If your dog already knows how to retrieve, skip to the "Exercise description" on page 60. Otherwise, read the following section on how to teach the retrieve or review the steps in the "Finding Lost Keys" section of Chapter 8.

Any dog can learn to retrieve

During the initial retrieve training, as with all other kinds of training, it is crucial to avoid saying the word "no" or punishing the dog, even if she does something you regard as wrong. You never know what your dog will associate your displeasure with. If you were to punish the dog for chewing an item she is to retrieve, she may become afraid to approach or retrieve that item in the future. If you are really unlucky, the dog may become afraid of you, because you are angry. Work to create a calm and friendly atmosphere for the training instead.

If you do wish to teach your dog to carry things by mouth, avoid any methods that include any element of punishment, pain or aversives. You want your dog to retrieve voluntarily and find it a pleasant experience to cooperate with you!

To begin, find something in or around the house that your dog will take her in her mouth voluntarily. Whatever it turns out to be (legal or forbidden!), this object will be the best starting point for the training. Get it and hold it in front of your dog. As soon as she grabs it with her mouth, praise and exchange it for a treat. If she doesn't want to take the object while you hold it, place it on the ground in front of her. Praise and exchange with a treat whenever she picks it up. The treats you use must be good enough for her to let go of the object to grab a treat in exchange.

Find something that your dog will willingly put in her mouth.

At this stage, you should position your hand so that your dog can easily place it there rather than on the floor. When your dog easily and willingly takes the object and then gives it to you in exchange for a treat, it is time to place the object further away from where you are standing. But do not throw it yet: just walk several feet and calmly put it on the ground. Now your dog must walk a few steps to fetch the object and carry it some steps back to you. Great! Praise and give a nice treat.

The next step involves throwing the object. Increase the distance you throw it slowly and gradually. If your dog starts to play and chew the object, start over again by calmly placing the object in front of her. Always change with a treat *before* your dog starts to chew or play. This is your responsibility, not the dog's. Slowly increase the distance of the retrieve gradually. Be careful to also limit the length of your training session, as long sessions may stress the dog, and stress increases the likeliness she will want to chew the object.

If you train too long, your dog may get fed up with it, or maybe too excited, which may lead to making mistakes. By increasing the distance too fast, you risk that she will get too excited and consequently will chew and play with the object instead of coming to you with it. You may very well play with the object together with the dog, but *after* she gives it to you.

Reluctance to retrieve

Some dogs show little or no interest in taking hold of an item with their mouths. If this describes your dog, try filling a sock with some very good treats and then secure it by tying a knot. Lay the sock in front of your dog. As the dog grabs the sock, praise her and exchange it for exactly the same treat which you put in the sock or open the sock and pick out a treat to give to her. Expect one or two socks will be destroyed in this process! This will not be the dog's fault, but yours if you are too late in exchanging for the treat. What the dog "buys" from you must be of higher or equal value in her eyes. And dogs are good at such assessments.

Repeat a few times, then take a break. Stop too early rather than too late. After some training, test if your dog will pick up a sock even when there is no food in it. Use the same sock initially, as it will smell of food. If your dog picks it up, give her a jackpot and be happy together. If she does not pick it up, put food in it again and continue on as described above. Gradually reduce the quantity of food in the sock, while always making sure you have some nice treats she can buy from you in exchange for the sock. Show your dog how rewarding it can be to pick up an empty sock as well!

When an empty sock scented with food works, try a clean one. When a clean one works, try something else. Gradually increase the difficulty of the object in terms of your dog's ability to pick it up. When you have warmed up two or three times retrieving something easy, all of a sudden you should drop a new object on the ground. If your dog picks it up or maybe only mouths it, praise and give her a jackpot. Eventually, you may reach the goal of having a dog who will pick up almost anything for you.

Chili retrieves a metal basket.

The more willing the dog is to pick something up, the easier it will be to train her to retrieve, so take the time to do some research that will teach you what your dog prefers. Some dogs love plush toys, while some fall for leather toys. Others may prefer rubber or wooden toys. Anything that is not harmful may be used. Over time, you can train your dog to grab hold all kinds of things: forks, coffee mugs, little coins, wine corks, heavy metal objects, buckets, the long handed scrubbing brush, even wallets and keys. Just let your imagination go and this will be a game of great fun for you both.

Another way to train a dog to retrieve is to follow the steps described in Chapter 8 (Finding lost keys and other items). Follow the steps from the very beginning, but rather than stopping when your dog paws the item, carry on until your dog grabs hold of the object with her mouth.

The Lost Retrieve—step by step

Exercise description. This exercise is similar to the Finding Lost Keys exercises (or other objects) described in the previous chapter. In that case, rather than finding a specific named item which you know you have lost, your dog will walk the route you just completed a second time and find and return to you any lost item. A win-win situation for sure: fun for your dog and helpful to you. The first times you do this, use a toy or other object that your dog really loves. Later, you can use anything, as long as you know your dog will retrieve it.

Goal. Your dog will be able to find and return to you any lost item along a route that you have just travelled with her.

First phase of the training.
Phase 1. Build up your dog's motivation.

1. Pick a place with some sort of path where there are a minimum number of distractions (people, other dogs, etc.). Walk your dog on leash along the path and stop at a peaceful place. Show your dog the toy (or other object) you have chosen and drop it on the ground while restraining your dog gently. Let her see but not touch the toy! For you, the rule here is that you can only hold the leash and under no circumstances can you say something like "No," "Leave it," or "Don't touch." Your goal here is to have the dog interested in the toy but have to wait a little bit before getting at it.

2. Now call your dog and invite her to follow you a few steps (dog steps!) away from the toy, moving backward

in the direction you approached this location. Back up as far as you can without her losing focus on the toy. Then let her loose to go fetch the toy. Join the party! Finish by exchanging the toy for a delicious treat.

3. The first few times you release your dog, do not give any cue. Only when you know she will fetch the toy do you give the cue.

4. Take a short break, allowing your dog to sniff and relax. The toy should be hidden in your pocket during your break. Then repeat Steps 2 and 3.

5. Now let the dog continue to watch when you drop the toy, but each time you do this you should walk farther away from it before letting her run to it. At this stage, make sure you "retrace" your footsteps after dropping the toy. This way, your dog is back-tracking both her own and your footsteps.

6. Repeat Step 5 two or three times in a row, then take a longer break for the dog to calm down and think about something else for awhile. To make sure your dog keeps the interest high, always stop to take a break when she is the most interested!

Phase 2. Hiding the toy.

1. Continue to keep dropping the toy while the dog is watching, but now walk away from it far enough that she cannot see it anymore before releasing her. Increase this distance each time you repeat this phase of the game. How fast you can increase the distance depends on your dog and how she works. Some dogs move through this phase quickly while others are slower. Some can find the toy at a distance of 50 to 60 yards quickly, while some will take much longer.

2. Now try dropping the toy so that it will be hidden by heather or other vegetation. If you are moving along a path, go past a curve before letting the dog loose to search.

Phase 3. Putting this behavior on cue.

1. Now that your dog runs for the "Lost Retrieve" without even seeing it, it is time to introduce a cue. "Lost" is what I use to say—in Norwegian, however! Pick a word that makes sense for you and that sounds different from any other cue your dog has learned. Say the word clearly and in a friendly manner to her as she starts to move at the very same moment you release her to go for the toy.

2. Repeat a few times to let the meaning of the cue word sink in. Repeat in a series of 1 to 5 repetitions.

3. Until now, your dog has watched you dropping the toy. To test if the cue really means something to her, you need to drop the toy without her seeing you do it. After secretly dropping the toy, walk a few steps back and give the cue. If your dog runs to get the toy, she understands the cue and the behavior. If not, you have to repeat the previous phase a few more times before making a new test.

4. In this test phase, you are only concentrating on the cue. Hide the toy rather close by, but not so close that the dog can see it immediately after she turns her head. If she can see it after having run a few steps, that is fine at this stage.

5. Now that your dog responds to your cue for "Lost," it is time to let her backtrack your single track. Do as before, only when you secretly drop the object, you continue in the same direction, without turning around as before. When you have reached a distance which is a little shorter than your dog is used to, turn around so that you and she are facing the direction of the toy, and give the cue as you release her. If this does not work, repeat this step a couple of times allowing her to observe when you lose the toy, and then it should be okay again.

Phase 4. Increasing the length of the search.

1. Start on this phase only when you have tested that the cue really gets your dog to work. Your goal now is to increase the distance back to where the toy is hidden while at the same time making sure that the dog does not see you "lose" something. If you train purposefully and regularly, your dog may be able to run up to a mile back to fetch something as small as a candy wrapper!

2. Repeat several times, continuing to increase the distance involved. Take notes of what you do and achieve! What you did last is easily forgotten, and thus you risk stagnating at a certain level.

3. Continue increasing the length gradually, until you think it is long enough for your purposes. Some owners might think 100 yards will be sufficient; others who hike with their dogs may want a distance of a mile or more. Whatever your goal is at this phase—even if your dog can go back long distances—give her a short run every now and then for variation sake. Don't always make it more difficult. Sometimes it must be easy to keep up your dog's motivation.

Phase 5. Difficulties along the route.

1. All paths are not straight, and some even have crossing paths which makes following a scent more difficult. Your dog should learn to handle this. The dog has already been there, after all—before you "lost" the toy— so a crossing should not be too complicated. Nevertheless, a crossing path may be a challenge for your dog and you should find one for her to practice dealing with.

2. The first time you ask the dog to search along a path with a crossing, place the toy only a couple of feet beyond the crossing point, not more. You may want to make sure the toy is large and attractive to make it easier for her. The difficulty here is not finding the toy, but choosing the right direction to turn at the crossing. When your

dog begins to choose correctly, gradually increase the distance from the crossing point to the spot where the toy is dropped. After a few repetitions like this, a crossing will no longer represent any real difficulty.

3. Another challenge for your dog may be meeting people, other animals or dogs along the route, especially if you have been training in isolated areas. If you decide to start this training where your dog will encounter people or other dogs, you will find that it may not be as challenging as you feared. You will need a helper for this step, who will act as a distraction. Since this distraction will make the Lost Retrieve more difficult, hide the toy a short distance away and choose an exciting toy. Keep the helper and the dog a good distance apart to avoid contact. If your dog does approach the helper, have him only turn away from the dog and remain passive, silent and boring. At first, you will need to experiment to see how far the helper and the dog need to be apart to avoid the helper being a distraction. In some cases, the helper will have to stay 200 feet out of the way and partially hidden in the woods. Once your dog can do the retrieve with a person placed 150 to 200 feet away from the route, start shortening the distance. Eventually, your dog will run straight past a person coming up the path.

4. For encountering other dogs on the route, repeat the same steps as with humans. The dogs you use should be calm and not too attractive to your dog. The more interest you think your dog will have in the other dog, the longer distance you need from the path to the other dog. Use toys of high value, and reinforce with really good treats when you have such heavy temptations for your dog.

5. Stop immediately when you have success. Do not "try once more because it went so well," because that is when it most often goes wrong!

Try training your dog in areas where there are distractions and competing scents to further test her skills.

Phase 6. Finding more than one item along the path.

1. One last variation of this exercise is to "lose" more than one object on the same walk. The first time you try it, allow your dog to watch what happens. Gently drop a favorite toy, walk three or four steps, and then drop another one. Walk about 25 feet more before sending your dog back for the toys. Praise and treat when she returns with the first one, and send her immediately back once more for the second toy. Praise and treat abundantly for finding toy number two!

2. Didn't find toy number two? Do it once more, but place the two toys closer to each other this time.

3. When your dog has learned that there may be more than one toy out there, start increasing the distance between them. Eventually, the first may be 30 feet away, while the second one is 250 feet away. As always, build the distance up gradually in steps of 6 to 10 feet, continually increasing the increments and overall distance as long as you want or as long as your dog succeeds at the game. Now you have a dog who can search hundreds of feet through the forest to fetch things you lost. Not bad!

Keep in mind

Plan the training so your dog always has success and keep it fun and varied. Gently drop a loved toy while your dog is occupied with something else, turn around and walk back until the toy cannot be seen anymore. Turn yourself and the dog back into the direction where the toy remains. Give the cue and release the dog. You know she will run some steps as this was tested in the fourth phase. Due to this, the best is that the toy lays only a little bit further away than what the dog will run. This way, it is likely that she will see the toy before she gives up, but still after having run a few metres. When you have done this a few times, your dog will run trustfully for the toy when you give the cue.

Even if you are not satisfied with how far your dog walks or runs to retrieve, I find it a bad idea to give the dog a cue for "Forward" to help her out solving this task. What you are working on now is not obedience training but a search game. If your dog does not run far enough when sent out for a Lost Retrieve, it is because the motivation is too low or because you are progressing too fast. Simply put, your dog is not completely trained. And in this case it is useless starting to train something else until she is.

Fant with my money: You can even train your dog to find and retrieve money!

CHAPTER 10

Pancake Tracking

The most fun I have in teaching puppy classes is when we have a tracking day. Puppies at the age of 10 to 12 weeks can be seen jumping happily and determinedly through the heather to find out what happened to that pancake!

Yes, pancake is what I wrote. Or a hot dog.

The very first track I will make for a dog—young or old—I create by tying up a pancake, hot dog or a lamb chop (or something else delicious) to the end of a rope and then pull it behind me as I walk. Hence the name "pancake track."

Any dog can follow a track—in fact it seems they are born with this ability—but nevertheless, we need to train for it. Why? Because we are not just training the ability to track, we are also building a high level of cooperation between dog and handler.

The beauty of the pancake tracking method is that the dog gets focused on what is jumping and bumping across the ground instead of just on the person that walks away. At the same time, the person disappearing ahead is someone the dog really wants to follow. This way, I can achieve something quite rare in dog training (and other circumstances as well)—killing two flies with one swat.

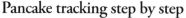

Pancake tracking step by step

I am going to use the example of pancakes for this exercise, but obviously most any kind of food will do. A hot dog on a rope, a waffle, a lamb chop, whatever. You might want to consult your dog on her preference!

1. What you need is a stack of pancakes and a string or rope six to ten feet long. For the dog you need a harness and a long tracking leash. Little puppies may very well do this off leash. You may also find a helper quite useful, someone who can drag the pancake along for you. Check on the wind direction before you start—the track should absolutely be laid with the wind, if there is any, at the track layer's back. Also, you must pick a location where the track layer can disappear out of sight of the dog after dragging the pancake no more than ten yards by moving into vegetation or around a hill or corner.

2. Put a harness and attach the long leash on your dog. Hold the dog on leash. Tie the pancake to the string and give the string to the helper. Your helper must show the pancake to your dog by putting it on the ground and pulling the string a little to make the pancake move. Let the dog almost catch the pancake. Play cat and mouse with it for a short while, but try hard not to let all the pancake end up in the dog's belly right away. This happens now and then: this is why you must have a stack of pancakes with you. It's actually a good thing if the dog manages to get a nibble of the pancake.

Let your dog observe the item being dragged across the ground.

3. As long as the pancake is visible to the dog, the helper drags it along the ground. Once out of sight from the dog, the helper can carry the pancake in his hands. Your job as the dog handler at this stage is to do nothing but hold the dog back. Allow the dog to go 2 to 3 dog steps forward in the direction of the pancake. Do not give your dog any commands or cues (such as "Sit," "Calm," "Wait" or anything else). If you attempt to encourage your dog by giving exciting little shouts or whispers, you only risk to withdraw the dog's attention from the pancake and over to yourself. Rather, remain passive and calm and allow your dog to keep looking in the direction of the pancake that walked away.

At this point, the track layer disappears into some vegetation.

4. Once the helper has disappeared from the dog's sight, have him walk in a curve, not in a straight line, avoiding sharp angles. After about 60 to 120 feet, he should sit and hide holding the pancake. If any pieces of the pancake fall off on the route, this just provides more motivation for the dog to keep tracking. If the entire pancake falls apart with none left on the string, your helper should have a spare pancake in his pocket so that there will always be a pancake waiting for the dog to act as a reward. If the helper cannot wait for your dog for some reason, he should drop the spare pancake and something that smells of him (t-shirt, hat, glove) at the end of the track. Then he should walk another 10 yards in the same direction, continuing the curve, and come back to the starting point without crossing or even coming close to his own track where he started. If possible, however, have the helper wait for the dog to find him.

5. After the helper has "disappeared," you and your dog should wait. It's fine if your dog wants to roam a little and sniff the path where you are. Allow this, but hold

onto the leash, and do not begin to talk to the dog, pet or play with her or give commands. You have to remain passive during this waiting time and restrain yourself from any encouragement or similar activity. Each time the dog returns to the beginning of the track, allow her to advance a couple of steps (dog steps!) by letting the leash slide through your hands, as payment for remembering where the track is. Repeat this pattern of restraint and letting the dog move forward every time she leaves the track and returns to it by herself. Make sure you keep a good hold on the leash so she cannot go far away from the track anyway. Continue to say nothing to her: neither praise her nor use a cue.

6. Once the helper is hidden and all is quiet, allow the dog to follow the track. The first one or two times you should not give her a cue. Just follow along behind and gently hold the leash so it can slide through your hand. The dog should walk 12 to 15 feet in front of you, allowing her to work without you stepping on her heels. Keep a normal walking pace. Do *not* run! When you think your dog is moving too fast, gently slow her down by holding a little firmer onto the leash. Whatever you do, do not help your dog in finding the helper and the pancake. If you do so, she will learn to trust you and not herself, and you will make no further progress.

Allow your dog to sniff while you make her wait before beginning to track.

Then see if your dog can follow the trail successfully in the vegetation.

7. In case you get totally lost or are convinced you are not on the track, it is better to interrupt the effort and walk back to the starting point and then have a new track made shortly afterward. If your dog does not find her

way—which happens sometimes—you just have to think about what may have gone wrong. Was the track too long? Vegetation too high? Did your dog refuse to cross a creek? Is she too tired and well fed? Change what needs to be changed, and give it another try, either right away, later the same day or some other day. Always move to a fresh spot when you lay a new track, to avoid the new track overlapping with the previous one.

8. When your dog finds the helper and the pancake, join the party, praise her and tell her how wonderful she is. You might even want to have some extra pancake in your pocket with which to celebrate.

9. A dog who has successfully followed several "pancake tracks" in the manner described above should now be given more challenging tasks! The first thing is to lay the track without the dog watching the pancake being pulled across the ground. It's time to take away the advantage that this training has given her. The best way to do this is to make a short track of some 60 to 90 feet long so that she didn't see you make. Start it at a path or road then onto vegetation so that you can easily remember where it is. It is a good idea to mark the starting spot by scratching deep in the ground with your feet or by hanging up a ribbon. Your dog should be wearing a harness and be on a long leash. Start a few feet from where the track begins and just walk towards it letting your dog sniff. Ideally, she should be in front of you. When she comes to the track, she will probably follow it, and your task is to follow her. Since it is important when trying something new that the dog succeeds, keep the track short.

10. If your dog cannot follow the track without seeing the pancake being pulled along it, make a double track to help her overcome this hurdle. First, have a helper make a short track (without pulling the pancake!), leaving some pancake and some interesting item(s) belonging

to the helper at the end of the track. Do *not* allow the dog to see this track being laid. Clearly mark where the track begins with ribbons or other markers. Once this first track is laid, the helper returns to you and your dog. Now have the helper make a new pancake-pulling-track within a safe distance (20 yards or more) to the first track, allowing the dog to watch this time. Have the dog track along this second path and, after having found the helper and the pancake and received a lot of praise, walk her directly to the beginning of the first track (which she did not see being laid). Allow your dog to sniff and check it out by herself. Do not say anything or try to help her in any way, as this will normally only impede progress. Most dogs will pick up this track rather quickly.

11. Once your dog can follow a track without having seen the pancake disappearing, you and she are ready for challenges like older and longer tracks. Older, meaning a longer time elapsed between when it was laid and when the dog tracks it. Do not make the track longer *and* older at the same time. See the Track Training chapter that follows for advice on fun challenges.

Keep in mind

Some dogs like to run side-to-side all the time instead of consistently following along a track. Let your dog do this, but anchor yourself as you stay behind her and hold the leash gently but firmly until she starts to sniff and follow the track again. As soon as you believe she is back on track, follow her. Always stand still when you think your dog is not following the track. Most dogs will become more accurate with some experience.

Note that each track you make must be on "fresh," unused ground, 20 yards or more away from the previously made tracks. You can do pancake tracking without a helper if you don't have one or if your dog will not follow a track laid by a stranger. In that case, you have to tether the dog to a tree or a post and then play the helper's role yourself while disappearing with a pancake on a rope. Once you are back with your dog, you act as the handler again and allow your dog to follow the track. Most dogs will be more motivated to follow a track laid by you rather than a stranger. Just make sure that your dog feels safe and remains calm when you have to leave her alone. You should, however, keep trying tracks laid by a stranger once in a while. Over time your dog should build up enough self-confidence and motivation so that she will track any stranger.

Glenshee's first tracks

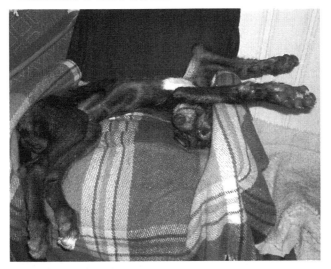

Glenshee sleeps after tracking.

My young Scottish Deerhound was presented to his first track at the age of four months. We were in the forest, along with my other dog, Troll. Glenshee and Troll waited by a tree while I pulled a colorful pencil case full of chicken after me into the woods. Glenshee tried to grab the pencil case when I started off and waited impatiently until I returned and he was allowed to pick up the track. The first time he was quite unsure and hesitant, but found the pencil case full of chicken after only 90 feet! He was presented with a new track immediately afterward, and this time he followed straight through the track in a determined manner directly to the chicken fiesta!

CHAPTER 11

Track Training

This chapter is not designed to be a complete course on tracking, nor will it cover the rules of competitive tracking tests. However, I will cover a number of aspects of tracking that hopefully make this fun activity easier for both you and your dog to learn and enjoy. If your puppy or dog is totally inexperienced in tracking, I recommend you go back to Chapter 10 and do the "Pancake tracking" exercises or read a basic book on tracking (See Bibliography).

Experienced or not, your dog is likely already more adept at tracking than you might believe. In fact, you might have seen her following tracks without you really noticing or being aware of it. For example, if you and family members are out for a walk with your dog, and one of your "pack" leaves the path for a reason and then returns, you might observe that the dog often checks out the route just taken with her nose to the ground. Your dog may frequently check out a route of another dog as well. Dogs are naturally curious and have natural talents in tracking.

Simply put, a track is a scent path created by the impact on the ground along which something or somebody has moved. Anything that moves along the ground leaves a track, whether it's a person, tractor, bike, moose, mouse or an even an insect. Scent can also be airborne in nature. Have you noticed that you can smell the scent of perfume when a person passes you on the street? Scent literally sticks to the environment.

Even if you cannot see any evidence of tracks, they exist. Not all imprints are visible to our eyes, but they are still there: vegetation is crushed; insects and other little creatures are killed and injured; the ground itself is compressed so that little pockets under the ground are squeezed and small amounts of gas or liquid is released. Even our human noses can smell broken vegetation (think of freshly cut hay in a farmer's field). When I walk in a bog, even my nose can detect the smell of the gas that is evaporating. Usually we do not smell anything from our own footsteps, however dogs can.

The tracks our dogs can smell have three major components:

1. Broken up, disturbed ground and vegetation. In a fresh track—normally one less than two hours old—the smell of disturbed ground is strong. It will be at its peak after 15 to 20 minutes, and then decrease over time as the "wounds" heal. The injuries on the plants will heal, the dead insects will be eaten or dry out, and the stream of gas or liquid that oozes out of the squeezed pockets in the ground will cease. However, it is the disturbed ground and vegetation that normally catches the dog's interest initially. Only later do they learn to sniff for the scent of the animal or human who created the track.

2. The scent of the species that created the track. This scent is formed by body particles and cells that are constantly falling off any animal or human as they move about. A person may "shed" hair, dandruff and body particles as small as a molecule from his body and clothes which then fall onto the track. Wild animals often leave hair, blood, feces and urine on the track in addition to small-er body particles. All of this provides clues to the dog who can learn to "read" the track as to whether it was a human, chicken, dog or even a bike that passed by.

3. Each and every individual has his own smell, similar in the way to fingerprints. So not only can a dog determine that a track was laid by another dog, your dog can read *which* dog it was. They can pick up information like age, sex, sexual status (heat!), and whether the dog was healthy or not, just to mention some examples.

It is wise to keep all of this information in mind while laying tracks. There is, for example, no such thing as an area which is absolutely devoid of tracks. Someone has moved there at some time. It may have been people, animals or a vehicle. Then you come along and lay your track on top of this, believing that "your" track is the only one there. But now you know. At least you have an idea on how much information might lie on the ground and will show some more patience with a novice dog checking all the smells. This is visualized on footsteps in the sand on the beach, or on newly fallen snow. And don't forget how dogs prioritize the use of their senses—scent comes *after* vision and hearing and you need to keep that in mind to succeed in creating a good tracking training program for you and your dog.

Tracking equipment advice

I have seen how unsuitable equipment can ruin an otherwise good tracking session, so let me give you some advice on this subject. Imagine having made a long and well-prepared track for your dog. The dog starts off perfectly and tracks beautifully. Then she loses the track while fighting her way through some heavy vegetation. Once past that hurdle, she works to find the track again, but meanwhile her long leash is completely stuck in a bush. You have to sort out the leash and the dog and start all over again, hoping to find your way back to the same track. An inexperienced dog may easily lose his motivation in all this mess.

So, the most important piece of equipment is a 15 to 30 foot tracking leash made out of rather stiff line that does not absorb water or cling tightly around trees. My tracking leash was purchased in 1988 and I guard it like a treasure! It never gets stuck in brush, just the opposite to what happens with most other leashes I have seen used. Ask experienced people what they recommend and then test them out for yourself to figure out what you prefer. In addition to being stiff and not water absorbent, it should not have a loop or a knot along the line. The best are all plain and smooth so they will not get stuck.

The tracking leash should be attached to a harness, not a neck collar. Buy a simple harness that fits your dog well so it will not cause any discomfort. The best idea is to bring your dog to the shop to try it on.

Tracking leash and harness in action.

Motivation, trigger and payment

The proper leash and harness are what you need in terms of equipment. But before you start to train, you must have something your dog wants to work for, some sort of payment. It can be a favorite toy, hot dogs, liver, meaty bones, chicken, steak, pankcake, cheese, even an apple. Ask your own dog what he or she prefers through testing. Even if your dog loves a particular ball, it may happen that she will prefer something else (preferably edible) as a reward for tracking. It is important for you to be aware of the dog's preferences to take advantage of them in training.

What I like to do in terms of rewards is to try to duplicate what would have happened on a successful track for a wild dog. The dog often follows a track which can be long and make her weary. Then the dog will catch, attack and kill the prey, usually eating it on the spot, napping, then eating more. So I pick a "payment" that will take some time and some effort to fetch and/or eat. A pig's ear, dry fish, a stuffed Kong, or a big meaty bone can all work well. For puppies and small dogs, an empty toilet roll with some food stuffed inside will do. Use your imagination and come up with something that takes time without being too difficult or discouraging.

Imagine being invited to help a friend paint his house. To lure you into this, he promises to take you to a restaurant and buy you a nice meal. When the house is painted, instead of treating you to a nice restaurant, he serves frozen pizzas. Even if the pizza is delicious and you like it, you have to admit that you feel that he has cheated you a bit, right?

It can work this way with dogs, too. If you have lured a dog into tracking using a ball, she will consider the chance to play with the ball payment for the task. She may view being paid with treats instead may be "cheating." The way you counter that is to let her have *both* the ball and some treats.

If you tease with a pancake at the beginning of a track, the pancake should be considered the trigger to tempt the dog to work. Finding the pancake in the track is the reward for a job well done, and is meant to increase the chances that the dog will follow a similar track another time. If you want to build up the dog's motivation to go tracking with (for) you, you have to provide some overlap between the trigger and the reward. Be predictable and reliable, and keep your promises!

Since most dogs will track a scent path laid down by a human, it is a very good idea that the person hides and holds the reward. In this case, the dog will not kill the track layer (of course!), but may regard this as a track that reunites a pack. I even bring a treat for myself, and my dog and I will have a nice party together.

Track laying: the role of the helper

I have no intention of providing a complete training manual for helpers here, but I want to give both helpers and trainers some advice to help avoid common mistakes. If you are asked to lay a track for a training mate, make sure you get careful instructions of what she wants. Likewise, when you as trainer or handler ask someone to lay the track for you, take the time to give careful and sufficient information to your helper.

Wait calmly with your dog as a helper lays the track for you.

I can still remember from my time as a beginner in utility obedience how much criticism we, the inexperienced, got when we made mistakes. Much of this criticism was not really fair, as the dog handler or instructor had failed to give sufficient information.

Have you ever noticed how difficult it is to walk straight forward in the woods or in a meadow? And what is an angle? Usually an angle means 90 degrees, but that must be made clear. Even if you know you are to make a right angle, the tendency is almost always to make them more open or larger than 90 degrees. Without a compass or having some sort of marker system, you will never make it.

Bearing this in mind, you can see how easily you can get off course. You are supposed to lay a track that extends 300 yards forward, then angle to the left and walk another 200 yards in the new direction, angle to the left again, then walk another 250 yards and establish the end of the track there. If you managed to follow the instructions carefully, you will end up about 200 yards from the spot you started off.

As a tracklayer, if you don't use a compass you will need to use land-marks such as a tree, a stone or something that is easy to recognise and provides you with a direction. If you can locate three landmarks, you can easily follow the right course. When you reach the first land-mark, make sure to pick a new one behind the last one, so that you always have three marks before you. To make a right (90 degree) angle, use three landmarks. One marks the direction you came from, the second one will be exactly the angle you need to turn, and the third will show the new direction. When at the point for the angle, turn to the direction you came from and double check all your land-marks to make sure that the angle you intend to turn is correct. Again, pick three marks to support your new direction, and carry on walking.

Placing objects on the track

As a track layer, you will sometimes be told to place objects on the track. These may include dog toys, food or other human possessions. Always drop or lay them down between your feet on the track—never throw them off to the side. The point is that the dog should react to things a person would have dropped in his tracks. Also, for a novice dog, objects should not be placed on or close to an angle in the track. Put the object about 75 feet before or after an angle. The item to be placed at the end should be something the dog values highly, like a dearly loved toy or an extra tasty piece of food. Some-times you may be asked to sit at the end of the track and wait for the dog, holding the food or toy. If not, place the final reward (normally together with some of your own stuff) on the ground and then walk another 5 to 10 yards in the same direction before you make a turn to get back where you want to go. Be very careful not to cross or come close to your own track and mess it all up!

Ribbons as markers

I prefer not to use ribbons or other markers along a track. This is be-cause the handler often fails to learn to trust the dog and only looks for ribbons as confirmation for being on the track. When you have learned to "read" your dog, it is easy to determine whether she is on the track or not.

Nevertheless, many people do like to use ribbons and in certain circumstances they can be useful. The key is that the markers must be visible to you, but not distracting to the dog. You need to take care while placing them while you are laying a track. If you want to place a ribbon on a tree or fence to mark a track, stretch your arm upwards so the ribbons will hang high. They should be easy to see from a distance, but be high enough not to disturb the dog. Avoid taking steps off the track to place the ribbons.

To increase the visibility and usefulness of the ribbons they should be relatively long and always placed in such a way that when standing next to a ribbon you should be able to see both the next and the previous one. Depending on the terrain you are using, it may be a challenge to use ribbons. When there are no trees or fences, you just have to improvise and put the ribbons or other markers on the ground or in the grass.

Rewarding the dog

Now let's focus on our behavior toward the dog at the end of track. Both novice and experienced dogs will enjoy finding a human friend on the track, especially in the initial training. But you should also frequently let the dog find people as she progresses onward also. This is the whole point of training for search and rescue, after all—to find people! Many dogs take great pleasure at finding someone at the end of the track, not just an object or food. A "family reunion" at the end of the track is close to the meaning of life for a family pet dog! You, as the reward, need to know if the dog prefers tug of war, cat and mouse play, treats or to be touched and how to be touched. Experiment beforehand so you know what she enjoys.

Humans and dog are celebrating the dog's success in rescuing a "lost" lady!

Of course, you may not know the dog well and you do need to train her to find a stranger if you are going to do search and rescue. In this case, it is important that you don't seem challenging or threatening when she finds you. Bend your knees rather than leaning over a dog. Don't stare. Never touch a strange dog over or around the neck. Don't hold the dog tightly or be rough with a dog you do not know. Finding you is supposed to be nothing but pleasant for the dog, not a challenge.

I hope this section of the chapter has given you a good outline of your task as a helper and track layer. The rest you will have to experience during training. Good luck, and enjoy your track laying.

Track training procedures

After following a few tracks using the procedures outlined below, your dog will have experienced that tracking to find a real person is exciting or that something good will be waiting for her somewhere along the track. And you will quickly learn what is easy and what is not so easy for you and your dog so you know what to work on going forward.

I have mentioned this before, but it is important that you change only one parameter or criterion in your training at a time. This means that only one element should be made more difficult for each track exercise. Imagine laying a track which is older and longer than the one before and is also in a totally new location. If, to your surprise, the dog fails to follow this new track to the end, you will not know whether it was the age, length or the new location of the track that was the problem because you changed three parameters, not just one. So this training session did not really show you anything useful. If the dog happened to succeed on this track, be happy that you are lucky and remember next time to change only one thing.

I am also going to assume here that your dog has worked on the "pancake tracking" exercises from the previous chapter and that she can now pick up and follow a track without seeing a pancake or other object being dragged along the ground or a person walking away into a forest or around a corner. In other words, these tracking exercises will be more challenging.

Two parameters you can use to increase the challenge are the age of the track and the length of the track—but not both at the same time. So, first you have to choose: age or length? The answer is not always straightforward. Normally, I will increase the age of the track first, especially for very eager and fast dogs.

Age of tracks

Is there an age of track so old that it is impossible for the dog to follow? In theory, yes, but it is hard to say. A student of mine who trained her dog to track for injured game animals reported that her Rottweiler could follow a blood track from a deer that was 125 hours old, a little more than 5 days! Impressive, isn't it? Others have mentioned a week, some even a month. I was told of a Bloodhound who could follow a track that was one year old, but I have been unable to confirm it as fact.

For practical reasons, the first few tracks for a young dog will be 4-10 minutes, just as long as it takes to make them. For them, the scent should be as strong as a freshly printed newspaper is to us. Once you have success in "pancake tracking," meaning that the puppy understands the game, you can wait 15 to 20 minutes before your dog is presented to the track. Most dogs can handle this easily, although some will find it difficult.

If your dog fails on a track of a certain age, make a new track right away and let it age to a point where she has succeeded before. If that works, reward her and take a break. In your next training session, start with a short track aged 5 to 10 minutes as a warm up, and then work your dog up to a new track that is aged 10 to 15 minutes older than the first one. Carry on like this until your dog easily follows a track aged for an hour. Whenever your dog fails, go back to a track age that she has mastered before and then try a longer aged track again.

Once your dog is successful on a one hour old track, increase the age of the track in increments of 20 minutes until she can handle a two hour old track. Continue to increase the age 20 to 30 minutes each time and don't hesitate to push the envelope a little. If it doesn't work, all you have to do is make a new track which is not so old, and again carry on increasing the age, but now in shorter steps.

Even when your dog can follow two hour old tracks, you have to give her fresher tracks now and then. Vary the tasks continually, and watch out for stagnation at a particular level.

Length of tracks

As you increase the age of your tracks, you should also increase the length—just not at the same time. Achieving success at 150 foot long tracks, while a nice early step, should not be your ultimate goal. Dogs can easily follow tracks of several hundred yards and eventually many miles.

For most dogs, you can probably increase the length of the tracks in increments of 150 feet. If your dog can follow a 150 feet long track with you hanging onto the tracking line, chances are that she can manage a 300 foot long track as well. Continue stretching out the tracks 150 feet at a time until at least 900 feet is "normal" for your dog.

After achieving 900 feet, you can try to increase the distance in larger increments, up to 300 feet. If the track gets too long for your dog, follow the same rule we used in ageing. Just create a new one that is shorter, and begin to build back up in shorter increments. Find a progression that works well and gives frequent success. You may need to keep the increments small, and then other times you can go directly from 900 to 1,500 feet. This depends very much on the day's conditions, and the dog's level of motivation and experience. It is all a question of keeping up your dog's motivation and physical condition as well.

Presenting challenges to your dog

The golden rule is that you should always keep challenging your dog a little, giving her gradually more difficult tasks. Most dogs enjoy these challenges. You might ask yourself if there is a point where you should stop challenging your dog, thinking that a certain level of performance is good enough. I like to think of it like this: without challenges, big or small, work easily gets monotonous and boring. So let's look at some challenges beyond track age and length.

There are many ways you can continue to challenge your dog while tracking, including more difficult terrain, a track that crosses a path, road or creek, a track that extends through a barn (think of all the interesting scents there!), or a track along a fence. There are so many possibilities. Just use your imagination.

Diego finds his way over some hindrances.

A track that crosses a well-travelled path will present your dog with some difficulty because it will likely contain so many tempting scent that your dog may follow a new scent trail on the path. A way to make this challenge easier is to ask the track layer to take very short and shuffling steps while crossing the path (this strengthens his scent) and along the first few yards after the path as well. Regardless, do-ing the opposite will make it more challenging. Of course, it is also a good idea to place a a small piece of food on the track a few yards after crossing the path to pay the dog for making the right choice. In fact, whenever you create a challenge, think about how you can reward the dog so that it counts (in the dog's opinion!) as payment for the particular challenge, and not for the track as a whole. This means that you may need to have several little payments en route in a single track.

Angled tracks

We humans tend to believe that angles in a track make them more difficult. This is why we usually lay all tracks out in a straight line when we start training dogs to track. The problem with this is, after just a few times, the dog learns that tracking with you means that the track will be straight and the task will not need much concentration and in fact may be visible to the dog. For this reason, I always lay tracks in the shape of a J or a U or L from the very beginning. That way I eliminate the possibility that the dog can find the solution by simply rushing straight forward instead of using her nose.

Once your dog has some experience, try to avoid a situation where the track is clearly visible to both you and your dog.

Early in training, I introduce several arcs and angles along the track. By making sure I always vary the tracks, I insure that the dog will have to use her nose every time. I also try to ask the tracklayer to vary the amount of scent on the track by stopping along the track to collect mushrooms or pick flowers which will cause the tracklayer to walk a little in this direction, then in the other, stand still for a while, and then walk a bit again, constantly changing directions bit by bit.

If your dog is moving too fast to sense an angle in the track or is just having problems following angles, you can try using ribbons to mark the angle. This will alert you to to when the dog is approaching the angle. Watch the ribbons. If you are 100% sure that the dog wants to go the wrong way, hold the line gently, but firmly (no jerks!), to stop her. Do not say anything, not "no" or anything else. Leave it to your dog to figure things out. Once she has picked out the right direction, let the line slide smoothly through your hand, and follow her. It is a good idea to have placed a nice payment 10 to 12 yards after the angle. If this is too difficult for your dog, break off immediately, call your dog and praise her for coming to you. This is no reason to be (or show that you are) disappointed. The only way forward at this point is to lay a new and easier track to keep up the motivation. When you do want to try an angle again, make it more gradual and then sharper and sharper.

Tracks walked on by others

These are tracks somebody has walked on *after* you laid it. Remembering how a dog prioritizes her senses, the most tempting and reasonable thing for the dog to do is to follow the most recently laid track. And in this case, that is the one "on top" of the one you laid and want your dog to follow. This can present a tough challenge for your dog.

When I start to train my dogs on tracks that have been recently walked on by others, I always choose relatively flat terrain with lots of usable landmarks and I will use ribbons in this case. I typically have a track layer making a track 50 to 75 yards long, marking it with red ribbons all along the way. After about 30 to 40 yards, the helper marks the crossing point by hanging up two red ribbons (or a red one and one of another color). Another 15 to 30 yards after this spot, the helper places the jackpot, and marks the spot with some extra red ribbons. (As usual, she must curve her way out without interfering with the track she just made.)

I then have another helper lay a second track crossing the first track at the spot with two ribbons. This crossing track should ideally hit the "red" track in a 90 degrees angle. The second helper marks her track using blue ribbons (at least another color than the original track). She is asked to mark the point where she crosses over the top of the original track with blue ribbons. So I end up with two very clearly marked tracks: a red one which the dog is supposed to follow, and a blue one which the dog will learn to ignore. When both track layers are back, dog and handler prepare for the tracking.

When the dog reaches the point at which the blue track crosses over the red one, she is likely to check it out in both directions. This is natural and you should allow this. Hold the leash in such a way that restricts the dog from walking more than 4 to 5 yards in the "wrong" direction. This is a situation where the use of ribbons is very handy. Once the dog is back on the right track (the red one), you follow. After a few more yards along the right track, she will find the jackpot as payment for her correct choice. Join the party, telling your dog how wonderful she is! Any dog that I have put through this exercise has learned it in a few tracks, with some in just two or three attempts.

To make this exercise even more efficient, set up a longer track (100 to 150 yards long) that is crossed by two or three tracks, each of them 30 yards or so apart. Place a treat about 10 yards after each crossing to reward your dog for making the correct choice to stay on the original track. Ideally, you should use ribbons as before, meaning you will need more than two colors. Most dogs will check the first crossing quite thoroughly, a little less on the second crossing, and very little, if any at all, on the third crossing. Dogs can learn very fast, if only we can prepare the right tasks for them.

Following a track that crosses a path walked on by people and animals makes the exercise more challenging.

Teaching the dog to find where the track begins

In some situations, neither you nor your dog will know exactly where a track begins, you may just have a vague idea. In this case, the dog will have to find the beginning of the track by herself. Up until now you have brought your dog directly to a starting point. Now you will teach her to find the track on her own (you, however, will know where the track lays).

To teach the dog to search for the track, I always start by having her attempt to find the track from the side, at roughly a 90 degree angle. At first, start close to the track and then make it more challenging. A typical progression might be a couple feet, then a few yards, working up to a 10 to 15 yard search for the track. If you are training for competition or for a search and rescue program, check out their requirements and train with these criteria as your *minimum* aim of performance. If you train your dog with your organization's minimum requirements, you will have no margin for error and the chances for failure will be high.

Cues

I dislike the word "command" when working with dogs. The English word "cue" is wonderful. Instead of sounding like a demand, it represents an invitation to cooperate and permission to work on something the dog has demonstrated she knows how to do. So the first key is to always wait to add a cue until you know for sure the dog knows what to do and will perform the task satisfactorily. When it comes to the tracking, I wait until she has tracked successfully at least 2 to 5 times without any kind of signal. Once the dog performs according to my expectations and starts tracking willingly, I introduce the cue "Track" immediately before she starts to walk and sniff into the track. You may pick any word you like, but avoid the word "Search," as most people will use that word for many other purposes as well. You need a different cue for different types of searching exercises.

New challenges

As mentioned before, creating new challenges for your dog will keep her motivated and learning. If you belong to a tracking club or team, you should have a lot of opportunities to come up with fun challenges. Make it a habit in your team to create surprising and entertaining tasks for each other. For example, create a birthday track where the objects hidden on the track are coins, dollar bill, or wrapped gifts, etc. Make sure some gifts are for the dog, too. Here are some more challenges to consider.

Age change tracks. Another good challenge is to lay a track where the track age changes in the middle. Send the track layer out with a book, a thermos and a sandwich. After a few hundred yards, have her sit down to read, eat and have her coffee or even take nap! After an hour or more, have her finish laying the rest of the track. What is interesting here is to see how (or if!) the dog has any reaction to the break and time change in the track.

If you wait long enough to age your track you might find conditions have changed. See if your dog can handle a track through fresh snow.

Lay tracks on a bicycle. The track layer begins a track in normal fashion until she reaches a spot where someone in your group has parked a bike. The track layer will walk with the bike first for about 25 yards, then get on the bike and ride slowly for about 100 yards. If the dog can follow this track successfully, have a big party for her and the tracklayer!

Tracks leading in the "wrong" direction. Lay a track that begins several yards off a dirt road or path, heading toward the road and crossing it before it continues on the other side of the road. Place the reward about 30 yards beyond where you crossed the road. If you lay the track for a friend, you should observe the dog handler as he and his dog start on the track. Many dog handlers will mistrust the dog when the dog wants to cross back over the road since most tracks starting on or near a road tend to continue away from it, not toward it. If you want this track to take longer to complete, then you just let it continue after the first intermediate jackpot, placing an additional jackpot (bigger) at the end of the track.

Rover in the dark

At a workshop in Germany, I met a dog who had lost his sight in a traumatic accident. He was totally blind, using his owner as a "guide human." He was very unsure and moved hesitantly and unwillingly on unknown ground. The first track we laid for him was roughly 10 yards long, made with short, shuffling steps and plenty of treats at the end. He sniffed on the track, but was anxious about moving forward in the unknown darkness. Consequently, he ended up moving around in circles without advancing in the track. His owner encouraged him and helped him forward until he reached the end and got his very well-deserved treat: a huge portion of chicken. This made him very tired and he had received a lot of support. Many hours later we laid another, similar track for him. This track was slightly shorter and we placed a tiny treat on it about every few feet. He still moved very hesitantly and still needed some help from his owner. But there had been a tiny trace of progress. The following day, he was given a new track of about 8 yards with chicken pieces every couple feet. This time he followed the track without any help, slowly but surely and safely until he reached the bowl with his reward. For Rover, this was the beginning of trusting himself and his own paws without being dependent on walking supported by a tight leash or the need to keep his muzzle in frequent contact with the back of his owner's knees.

CHAPTER 12

Training Scent Discrimination

A dog who has been taught scent discrimination can be used to detect a large number of distinctive smells (distinctive to her, of course!) from gluten, soya or traces of peanuts in your food, chanterelles in the woods and even explosives in an airport. While I will be using peanut oil as an example in this chapter, you can use the same steps to teach your dog to scent your keys, carrots, mint tea, leather gloves or whatever. All you have to do is get a sample of what you want the dog is to learn to search for. Pure gluten can be purchased in health shops, oils in food shops and pharmacies. If you want her to find mushrooms, you may have to go into the woods and find them where they grow.

What is "scent discrimination?"

Simply put, it is the ability to discriminate between smells or to pick one scent out among a number of others. For example, a drug dog trained to locate the scent of a certain drug will ignore the scent of food, sweat, leather, oil, tobacco and practically anything else in the vicinity. If you have competed in obedience, you may have some experience in this in the test in which the dog must find a small object that has the owner's scent among a group of objects. A dog's nose is very capable of this. Border patrol dogs in South Africa were used for years to recognize explosives, narcotics, rhino horn, rhino horn juice and ivory.

12 — TRAINING SCENT DISCRIMINATION

Introduce your dog to the scent of whatever it is you want her to search for.

Your dog's marking/reporting behavior

If your dog has learned how to find mushrooms in the forest, explosives in a suitcase or peanut oil in your food, it does not help you unless the dog has a way of communicating that fact to you. She must have a way to "report" or "mark" the presence of the scent so that you will understand what was found and where. The marking behavior may be almost anything, depending on what the dog is searching for and the surroundings she is working in. Police dogs finding criminals will normally be trained to bark. Dogs finding people in a collapsed building can mark by scratching the ground and/or barking. Land mines are marked by the dog sitting or laying motionless next to the mine. For something as harmless as mushrooms, you can teach your dog to sit, bark or come back to fetch you to indicate a find.

This dog has been taught to sit as a way to mark a find.

Regardless of what marking behavior you choose, it must be trained in advance. Your dog should have a reliable and happily offered bark, sit, down, retrieve, play bow or whatever. The training should be done exclusively with positive reinforcement and not with the use of punishment, force or any aversive consequences. Retrieves trained by force are absolutely useless. My experience is that behavior which is shaped is a great choice. Another very good option is to just wait and see what your dog offers by herself!

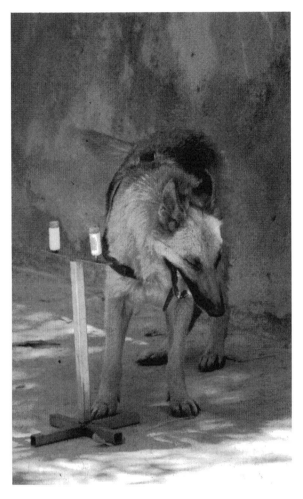

Kwanza has found a mine, but hesitates to offer her marking behavior.

Problems with marking

In the photo above, Kwanza, a mine detection dog in Angola, has found traces of explosives. She is trained to report this by offering a sit. Instead, she stands still displaying a long series of calming signals: yawning, looking away, turning away, freezing, blinking and paw lifting. Why? She is calming herself and her old negative associations. But she is also not moving away. Why not? Well, she knows she will get a reward for finding a mine, which she probably wants.

The explanation for her behavior seems to be this: she does not wish to sit because she was originally trained to sit by her handler jerking the choke chain at the same time as she was pushed down by a hand on the hip. While she has been working finding mines for two years, this reluctance to sit continued to pop up. The solution? We took her out of operational work and retrained her to sit with positive reinforcement. The cue had to be changed as well. After a couple of weeks, she was back on stage marking mines with a sit. It is possible that the problem may occur again later, but at least the dog handler now knows how to cope with it.

Obtaining the scent

In order to train scent discrimination, you must get access to it for training. Different scents can present a variety of challenges. You may understand the problem in training scent discrimination with peanut oil: it floats and it cannot just be placed down anywhere. Rather, you have to pour some into clean tin cans or jam jars. Paper or plastic cups may also be used—as long as you throw them away when done since you cannot remove residual scent from them.

I place 2 to 3 drops of oil into the container of choice. Jars or cans with narrow openings may be handy, since it will prevent the dog from trying to consume the oil. All of the containers you use should be identical both in size and color to prevent the dog from solving the problem by just looking at the container. Mark the containers to avoid mixing them up and to eliminate contamination problems. Bear in mind that the labels and the pen also will emit some scent (and the dog can see it, too), so you must have labels and markings on all the cans you use. When finished, clean all the containers just to be safe and start over.

Getting started with the training

Scent discrimination is a discipline consisting of several related parts: (1) the willingness to search; (2) training a marking behavior and; (3) learning what to search for. In many cases, a particular search pattern will be advisable. In all cases the dog must the have desire and confidence to work together with you. Remember, I will use the scent of peanut oil in the step-by-step training process below, but the steps would be the same regardless of which scent you choose.

As mentioned above, you will need to decide (or, through experimenting, let your dog decide) what marking behavior you want to establish when a find is made (bark, sit, etc.). If your dog is clicer trained, use your clicker for this game. If not, praise and treat. So, whenever I write "click" or "praise" you can choose which method you and your dog prefer. And the click/praise must immediately be followed by a treat. Like other kinds of training, scent discrimination is best taught by breaking it into small, achievable and measurable steps. You can move on from a given step when your dog is successful 80% of the time. If not, take a step or two backward.

Scent discrimination step-by-step

1. The goal here is to establish a positive association with peanut oil for your dog. Hold a container with peanut oil in it in front of her and click or praise immediately when she sniffs at it. Gradually hold the can further away, so that she has to take some initiative to be able to sniff the oil. Try leaving the container on the ground, letting her take a few steps toward it. Repeat this a few times until she goes directly by herself to the container with the oil to earn a reward.

Praise as soon as your dog sniffs at the scent you have chosen to work on.

2. The goal here is to get the dog to mark her find. You should work to have the scent of peanut oil become the cue for the marking behavior. Present the peanut oil to the dog. When she sniffs it, delay half a second before praising/clicking, and give the cue for the unwanted behavior (sit, bark). Reward even if the dog does not sit or bark because you need to be aware that there is a lot on your dog's mind right now! After a few times, the dog will begin to respond to your cue for the marking behavior.

An alternative way to get the marking behavior you want is to warm up by training the marking behavior immediately before the search work starts. With your enthusiasm for the chosen behavior fresh in mind, the dog will tend to offer this particular behavior to please you again and thus make you supply more treats! As always, make sure you only train in sessions of 5 repetitions and then take a break. Repeat this step until the dog marks spontaneously when she sniffs peanut oil.

3. The goal here is to teach the dog that only peanut oil counts, and that any other scent is to be ignored. Present two containers, one with peanut oil and one with sunflower oil to the dog. Arrange them so the peanut oil container is closest to the dog. Click for sniffing the peanut oil. Don't worry right away about the marking behavior. Ignore any sniffing at the sunflower oil (the "negative" scent). Whatever you do, keep yourself from saying "no" or "wrong" or "different" to the dog. If the dog won't leave the wrong oil, get a helper to hold the containers and hold the wrong can behind the helper's back. As soon as the dog sniffs the right oil, give her a jackpot! Now repeat this until the dog sniffs the peanut oil consistently, does the correct marking behavior, and ignores the sunflower oil. This is a big step forward, so do as many repetitions (with breaks) as needed here.

This Cavalier is being asked to choose the right scent from two containers.

4. Now we want to increase the challenge the dog faces in picking the right scent. At this point, select three containers, one of which contains peanut oil and the two others different scents. Once again, ignore any interest towards the "wrong" oils and click/praise (maybe Jackpot!) when the dog goes to the right one. You must continually change the positions of the cans for each attempt, otherwise your dog is likely to outsmart you (she is smarter than you think!). Repeat until she easily ignores the two negative scents, selects the peanut oil and performs the desired marking behavior.

5. Now, your goal is to get the dog to search six containers and find the one with the peanut oil scent. As the dog is successful, gradually increase the number of containers. Dogs employed to do this work in airports and similar places usually have to demonstrate they can find the right scent coming from six to eight alternatives. You may place the containers in a row or in a group or circle. Repeat until the dog easily and happily picks out the one correct scent from 6 to 8 choices.

This dog is trying to find the right scent under four containers.

6. This step involves a "negative" search for the first time—a search where no peanut oil is present. The goal is for the dog not to give any false markings but rather report to you that "there is nothing here!" First, present only one or two containers with other oils, and click when the dog *leaves* the last can! Gradually increase the number of containers to 6 or 8. Ignore false markings, but in case they occur, reduce the number of containers, making it easier for your dog. This is a step where the timing of your praise/click may be critical. Only

click immediately *after* the dog has left the containers. Little-by-little delay the click/praise further, until the dog comes all the way back to you when no peanut oil is present. Don't do many negative searches in a row. Vary it so that after one, two or three negatives on a row, your dog has a few runs where she finds the real thing. Repeat until the dog makes no more mistakes!

7. Now you should work on building your dog's endurance, i.e. how long you want her to work before a break is given. Do not demand too much at first and increase the duration very slowly. Observe her capabilities carefully, as it can be harmful to let her overdo the work. Make your plan so that it is not only a gradual increase, but let some periods be shorter as well. Be aware that every dog will have a different limit for endurance. Repeat until you have found the endurance level for your dog—one that ensures the dog is working willingly and efficiently.

8. Generalize the search work. You probably started the training in a peaceful place with few distractions. Now is the time to determine if your dog can search in other places with a variety of people, sounds and other disturbances present. Imagine a real life situation: you need to determine for health reasons if peanut oil is present in any food you might purchase from a grocery store or eat at a restaurant. While practicing at home is a good place to start, at some point you should try to arrange with the owner of a restaurant or the manager of a supermarket the chance to train in their stores. When your dog is comfortable working in one environment, change to a new one. Repeat until your dog works well in distracting new environments that are relevant to you.

9. At some point in the training process, you will want the dog to start working at a given cue. You may add the cue at an earlier stage, but you must never add the cue unless you know for sure that she will perform satisfactorily.

My little test for whether to add the cue or not is to prepare a training session, and when the dog performs two or three times in a row, I give the cue the third or fourth time. You really want to avoid the situation where you give the cue and the dog does not perform. Every time you call "come" and she does not come, the meaning of the cue loses value. That is why I am so adamant about this. Give the cue in a well-known environment the first few times, and go back through all the previous steps— the first couple times without a cue, then with the cue, in each new environment. Repeat until the dog always responds satisfactorily to this cue. Good luck!

Move outside and present your dog two new items to check out. This dog has chosen successfully.

10. The final step in scent discrimination is that you must learn to trust your dog. You may have noticed that so far in all of the previous steps you know where the scent is located and/or if there is any scent at all. In the real

world, you will not have this information, since that is why we started to train dogs for this in the first place! You need one or more helpers to prepare scenarios for you and your dog. Initially, it may be a good idea that your helper has the clicker or gives the verbal praise and you give the treat, but very soon you should handle it all yourself. One difficulty you may encounter is that you may have unconsciously been directing your dog in some way to show her where the scent is (or is not), either by slowing down, holding your breath or even fiddling with the leash. Working with a helper will negate that possibility and ultimately confirm that you have learned to trust your dog!

A fully trained "peanut oil dog"

Even when you have completed all of the above steps successfully, you are only at the beginning of the work involved to get a fully trained peanut oil dog. Peanut oil occurs in food in various forms and concentrations. Further training will be needed using food that is prepared with or contains peanut oil and food that is guaranteed to be free of it. Research all the different situations in which the oil may be present. For example, with meat, you will need to work with fried, baked and boiled meat, bearing in mind that meat or fish fried in oil may be irresistible temptations for your dog! To keep up the motivation for the search work, the reward must be as good as or better than what the dog is supposed to search for, so she will leave without eating it!

And remember, you are not allowed to yell at or punish your dog for any mistakes. Mistakes only occur when your preparation has not been good enough. Besides, you will never really know whether your dog is right or not in its marking, will you?

Some final advice

The most common trap to fall into is to give attention to the dog when she is sniffing the wrong/negative oils. Any attention, positive or negative, is likely to be interpreted by your dog as a reward, and you end up teaching her to mark falsely. Attention may be pulling at the leash, saying "no," laughing or even sighing. Instead of giving a negative reaction to a wrong behavior, you have to ignore it!

With dogs working independently like this, you need a dog who is very self-confident. Both in Angola and South Africa during my work there, I saw good mine detection dogs being severely set back or even completely ruined by being punished for false markings. This is a sure way to ruin a dog's confidence, both in you as well as in herself.

Accurate and correct timing of the praise (click) will be decisive for what the dog learns. If you praise for approaching something, the dog's interest for this will increase. But if you praise when the dog is about to leave something, the dog will learn to leave it alone. Observe your dog and her behavior carefully!

Keep a training diary. I do not know how many times my pupils (in many countries) and I have discovered how repetitive our training was until the day we started taking exact notes about what we really did. We *thought* that we are doing things differently, but we tended to act according to the same old patterns! Many have also discovered that the same problems often occured at the same time of the year, and this, too, was not clear until they started to keep a diary.

The ultimate reward of nosework is building a great relationship with your dog.

Sources and Resources

Note: This list includes works cited in the book as well as recommended reading.

About Track Laying. Betty Mueller, Howln Moon Press, 2001.

Click N Sniff: Clicker Training for Scent Discrimination. Deborah Jones, Howln Moon Press, 2001.

Din Hund fortsätter Beteende–inlärning–moment. (Your Dog the continuation: behaviour, learning, elements.) Järverud, Svend og Järverud Gunvor af Klinteberg, Solna: Naturia Förlag, 1986.

Din Hund praktisk hundebok. (Your Dog: a practical handbook) Järverud, Svend og Järverud Gunvor af Klinteberg, Wennergren-Cappelen AS, 1986.

Don't Shoot the Dog. Karen Pryor, Bantam Books, 1999.

From Leadership to Leading Role (lecture). Kristin Meitz Bru and Silje Kittelsen. Oslo, Norway, 2002.

Kantarellsök med Hund. (Searching for chanterelles with your dog.) Hallgren, Anders og Hallgren, Marie Hansson, Vagnhärad: Jycke-Tryck AB, 1990.

K9 Scent Detection. Jan Kaldenbach, Detselig Enterprises, 1998.

Lads Before the Wind. Karen Pryor, Sunshine Books, 2000.

On Talking Terms with Dogs: Calming Signals, 2nd edition. Turid Rugaas, Dogwise Publishing, 2006.

Tracking from the Ground Up. Sandy Ganz and Susan Boyd, Show-Me Publications, 1992.

Try Tracking: The Puppy Tracking Primer. Carolyn Krause, Dogwise Publishing, 2005.

INDEX

finding lost items, 5, 37–48,
49–55
naming your dog's toys and,
32–37
roles of tracklayers and, 81
search for, 27–31
olfactory sense of dogs, 5–6, 8

P

pancake training, 67–75, 85–86
patience, 11
peanuts, detection of, 100–109
people, search for, 5
plants, 77
play
as reinforcements, 17, 20
Square Search and, 38
positive associations, 13
progression, speed of, 20
Pryor, Karen, 15
punishment
learning by association and,
13
scent discrimination and, 109

R

reinforcements
learning by association and,
13–17
marking behavior and, 98
motivation for learning and,
79–80
track training, basics of, 83
reliability of behavior, 18
repetitions, 17–18
reporting behavior, 97–100
retrieve behavior

finding lost items and, 51–52,
56–66
problems with, 45, 58–60
reinforcements and, 98
Retrievers, 15, 24
rewards. See reinforcements
ribbons, 73, 82–83, 90–91
Rottweilers, 48, 85

S

scent discrimination, 77–78,
96–109
scent path, defined, 38, 76–77
Scottish Deerhounds, 75
Search for Treats exercise, 21–26
Setters, 24
shaping, 17, 98
situational leadership, 8
Square Search, 37–48
stress, avoidance of, 45
Swedish Bouvier des Flanders,
55

T

terrains, 44–45, 77
toys
Hide and Seek exercise and,
27–31
Lost Retrieve and, 61
naming, 32–37
as reinforcements, 14–15
retrieve behavior and, 59–60
training preparation and, 11
track training, basics of
preparation for, 11–20, 76–84
procedures, 84–95
tracklayers, roles of, 80–82
training diary, 109

treats
  choice of, 11
  as reinforcements, 14–17
  search for, 21–26
  Square Search and, 38
truffles, detection of, 5
trust
  importance of, 8
  scent discrimination and,
  107–108

U
utility obedience classes, 81

V
variable reinforcements, 16
vegetation, 77

W
weather, 44–45
wind, 43, 46
wolves, 7–8

Selected Titles From Dogwise Publishing
www.dogwise.com 1-800-776-2665

BEHAVIOR & TRAINING
Barking. The Sound of a Language. Turid Rugaas
Bringing Light to Shadow. A Dog Trainer's Diary. Pam Dennison
Canine Behavior. A Photo Illustrated Handbook. Barbara Handelman
Canine Body Language. A Photographic Guide to the Native Language of Dogs. Brenda Aloff
Chill Out Fido! How to Calm Your Dog. Nan Arthur
Do Over Dogs. Give Your Dog a Second Chance for a First Class Life. Pat Miller
Dogs are from Neptune. Jean Donaldson
Oh Behave! Dogs from Pavlov to Premack to Pinker. Jean Donaldson
On Talking Terms with Dogs. Calming Signals, 2nd edition. Turid Rugaas
Play With Your Dog. Pat Miller
Positive Perspectives. Love Your Dog, Train Your Dog. Pat Miller
Positive Perspectives 2. Know Your Dog, Train Your Dog. Pat Miller
Stress in Dogs. Martina Scholz & Clarissa von Reinhardt
Tales of Two Species. Essays on Loving and Living With Dogs. Patricia McConnell
When Pigs Fly. Train Your Impossible Dog. Jane Killion

HEALTH & ANATOMY, SHOWING
An Eye for a Dog. Illustrated Guide to Judging Purebred Dogs. Robert Cole
Another Piece of the Puzzle. Pat Hastings
Canine Massage. A Complete Reference Manual. Jean-Pierre Hourdebaigt
The Canine Thyroid Epidemic. W. Jean Dodds and Diana Laverdure
Dog Show Judging. The Good, the Bad, and the Ugly. Chris Walkowicz
The Healthy Way to Stretch Your Dog. A Physical Therapy Approach. Sasha Foster and Ashley Foster
It's a Dog Not a Toaster. Finding Your Fun in Competitive Obedience. Diana Kerew
Tricks of the Trade. From Best of Intentions to Best in Show, Rev. Ed. Pat Hastings
Work Wonders. Feed Your Dog Raw Meaty Bones. Tom Lonsdale

Dogwise.com is your complete source for dog books on the web! 2,000+ titles, fast shipping, and excellent customer service.

Made in the USA
Middletown, DE
29 May 2017